D0933700

"Susan R. Pitchford has penned (or at least word processed!) a new book with a master's touch in *God in the Dark*. Coming from a Franciscan orientation, she has tapped into a broad spectrum of the ancient mystical heritage of Christianity in a way that speaks to the average person in a fast-paced, modern world. Readers will find it a fine addition to their modern mystical books or a great introduction to the mystical tradition for new seekers and first-time readers."

> — John Michael Talbot
> Founder and Spiritual Father
> The Brothers and Sisters of Charity
> at Little Portion Hermitage

"Many Christians play it safe by practicing a tepid, no-risk spirituality in which we domesticate the roaring Lion of Judah into a nice, safe pussycat. Susan Pitchford's beautifully written book reminds us that an authentic relationship with God, others, and self depends on an embrace of whole-bodied desire on the one hand and the possibility of suffering on the other. This is a book that liberates us to let God be both the passionate Lover and the Roaring Lion God is."

> — Kerry Walters
> Author of *The Art of Dying and Living*

"In an accessible style, laced with rich metaphors, wry humor, and down-to-earth explanations, Susan Pitchford guides the reader to a fresh knowledge and appreciation of the Christian mystical journey. Since mysticism is about relationships, it inevitably involves passion (the enemy of boredom and apathy), whose two faces are desire (God desires us infinitely more than we desire God) and suffering (life's pain can be understood in positive, life-giving ways).

"Pitchford advocates a return to the mystical metaphor of the spiritual marriage in a twenty-first century framework—an evocative, potentially enriching challenge. Intimacy with God is viewed in an inclusive way that resists the attitude that one size fits all. Rather, mysticism is a way of intense prayer open to all the baptized called and willing to follow the path of desire for God in their daily lives.

"Pitchford takes a balanced approach to affirmative and negative prayer forms, but she focuses on the positive or kataphatic way, which she believes has been neglected. Her favorite exemplars include her 'spooky sisters'—medieval beguines such as Beatrijs of Nazareth, Hadewijch of Brabant, Mechthilde of Magdeburg and Marguerite Porete; Teresa of Avila and Mother Teresa; Francis of Assisi and John of the Cross. This book is an antidote to contemporary cynicism and indifference, a goad to those who desire to infuse their spirituality with new life and vigor."

— Elizabeth A. Dreyer
Department of Religious Studies
Fairfield University, Fairfield, Connecticut

God in the Dark

Suffering and Desire
in the Spiritual Life

Susan R. Pitchford

Foreword by Alan Jones

LITURGICAL PRESS
Collegeville, Minnesota

www.litpress.org

Cover design by Ann Blattner.

Excerpts from *Mechthild of Magdeburg: The Flowing Light of the Godhead*, translated by Frank Tobin. Copyright © 1998 by Frank Tobin. Paulist Press, Inc., New York/Mahwah, NJ. Reprinted by permission of Paulist Press, Inc. www.paulistpress.com.

1	2	3	4	5	6	7	8	9

Library of Congress Cataloging-in-Publication Data

Pitchford, Susan.
    God in the dark : suffering and desire in the spiritual life / Susan R. Pitchford.
      p.   cm.
    Includes bibliographical references and index.
    ISBN 978-0-8146-3351-9 (pbk.) —
    ISBN 978-0-8146-3942-9 (e-book)
      1. Spiritual life—Christianity.   2. Desire for God.   3. Suffering—Religious aspects—Christianity.   I. Title.

BV4817.P58 2011
248.4—dc22

2010048843

To Bob

for sticking through
the dip in the U.

Contents

Part II: Suffering

Part III: Union

Abbreviations

All Scriptures quoted in the text, except for verses from the Psalms, are from the New Revised Standard Version (NRSV), unless otherwise noted. The King James Version (KJV) is the default version for the Psalms.

Other versions used include the following:

ASV   American Standard Version
GNB   Good News Bible
Holman   Holman Christian Standard Bible
MSG   The Message
NASB   New American Standard Bible
NKJV   New King James Version

Acknowledgments

Jesus never wrote a book, a fact that's apt to make an author reconsider. It does seem, however, that some of his best friends have been writers, and I hope that he's had a hand, at least, in this one.

When I started doing talks on the spiritual life a few years ago, after my first book (*Following Francis*, Morehouse, 2006) came out, people seemed to connect to Franciscan spirituality, showed interest in experimenting with a personal rule of life, and were kind enough to laugh at my jokes. But it was when I talked about Francis' peace and joy during times of suffering and darkness that they really sat up in their chairs. Many of them seemed to think that these experiences were signs of failure and abandonment, whereas I've tended to take it for granted that suffering grief and loss is the risk you take when you love someone deeply. So I began to think that a book that examined the connection between love and suffering might really help people. I hope that will prove to be true, but in the meantime, my first thanks must go to those dear people whose courageous and hopeful struggles inspired this project.

I've had three spiritual directors during the time this book was percolating, and I want to thank each of them: Allan Parker, the consummate cheerleader; Valerie Lesniak, who gave me permission to go deeper; and Kathryn Ballinger, who understands the desires of my heart. Thanks also to my Franciscan brothers and sisters, especially the Seattle Fellowship of St. Clare. Being part of this community is like being surrounded by icons, each one a window into God. Several wise women have read and responded to parts of this work: Judith Gillette, TSSF; Chris Cowan, TSSF; and Teresa DiBiase, Obl. OSB—dear friends and powerful women, who know all the back roads. I take responsibility for any and all wrongheadedness that remains. Thanks also to Edie Burkhalter, TSSF, for being a spooky sister who is *not* dead. My parish, Christ Church Seattle, is blessed with excellent preaching, and I'd especially like to thank Fr. Steve Garratt, Frank Shirbroun, Obl. OSB, and Mary Whiting, whose sermons I've cited.

I owe an immense debt of gratitude to my agent, Kathleen Davis Niendorff; without her knowledge, skill, and energy this book would just be taking up space on a flash drive. The whole team at Liturgical Press have been a joy to work with, especially Hans Christoffersen, Mary Stommes, Stephanie Lancour, and Stephanie Nix.

Finally, my deepest thanks, as always, go to my family: Bob and Danielle Crutchfield, Nancy, Lynn, and Kim Pitchford. They all love me no matter how strange I am, and are mostly laughing with me. I think.

Foreword

"There be in God, some say, a deep but dazzling darkness." The seventeenth-century poet Henry Vaughan expresses a vital truth, which is explored with intelligence, passion, and humor by Susan Pitchford. In spite of her disclaimers to be a theologian, her book is a discerning work of the moral and theological imagination. It is an exploration well suited for our times, marked as they are by both shallowness and fierceness in religion. How do you tell the truth—the whole truth—and end with some good news? She writes in the tradition of another truth-teller, Annie Dillard, who pointed out some years ago the strange way we go about "saying our prayers." Dillard wondered whether anyone had the foggiest idea what sort of power we so blithely invoke when we pray. We're like children playing on the floor with our chemistry sets, "mixing up a batch of TNT to kill a Sunday morning."

The God of *God in the Dark* is passionate and intractably mysterious. And because we are all made in that divine image, so we too are driven by passion to embrace the unknown. True spiritual life has this erotic quality—marked by a longing that only God can fill. The spiritual life, then, as the poet Dante brilliantly understood, is concerned with the ordering of desire, the sorting out of our disordered loving. Given the immense and far-reaching consequences of the misdiagnosis of ourselves as consumers, it is no wonder that much of our religious sensibility has been reduced and commercialized. Spirituality isn't a "product." It can be neither bought nor sold, and Susan Pitchford skewers this misunderstanding with down-to-earth, accessible writing, marked with humor and honesty. The book is refreshing and yet stands in a long mystical tradition. The author reminds us why we were born—fire! This book is a great gift for a floundering, atomized culture—water in the desert.

Alan Jones
Dean Emeritus of Grace Cathedral
San Francisco
Honorary Canon of the
   Cathedral of Our Lady of Chartres

Preface

> Certainly it is necessary to [write this book] before reaching completely the estate of freedom, of this I have no doubt. And yet, said the Soul who wrote the book, I was so foolish at the time I wrote it . . . when I put into words something precious which could neither be done, nor thought of, nor spoken of: as if you wanted to enclose the sea in your eye, carry the world on the point of a reed or illuminate the sun with a lantern or a torch. Yes, I was even more foolish than someone who tried to do such things.
>
> —Marguerite Porete, *The Mirror of Simple Souls*[1]

This is not a book for theologians. Not that I would discourage them from buying it if they want to; my publisher would frown on that. But in writing on the roles of suffering and desire in the spiritual life, I am not attempting a scholarly opus that would draw together all that the theologians and mystics have said on these subjects over the millennia. I am not proposing to synthesize all that is known about these questions and then offer some stunning new insight. The aim of this book is much more modest than that.

What I've undertaken in this work is a little book for beginners, or near-beginners, that explores the ways of God with the human soul. My intention here is to do what Wendy M. Wright refers to as "messing around in a part-scholarly, part-prayerful way"[2] with some of the central themes of Christian faith. I specifically want to examine the centrality of *passion* to the soul's relationship with God, and of suffering and desire as the two faces of passion. Various writers have emphasized one or the other of these, and certain saints and mystics have seemed to lean in one direction or the other. Francis of Assisi is known as a joyful saint and is often shown dancing, while John of the Cross is seen as an austere, somewhat frightening saint best known for his writing on the dark night of the soul. Yet I've said that saints and mystics *seemed* to lean one way or the other, because in truth, Francis knew periods of deep darkness and suffering, and John's poetry overflows with the joy he knew in union with God.

In our day, many teachers of prayer emphasize one side of the spiritual life to the neglect of the other. Some see it as a succession of holy joyrides, measuring the success of prayer, and of Christian life in general, by the frequency and intensity of visions, voices, sensations, and other "events." This emphasis produces a shallowness in which our loyalty and commitment are based on feelings, like the seedling that has no deep roots and is scorched as soon as the sun hits it (Matt 13:20-21). Other teachers, reacting to this danger, urge people to disregard all thoughts, feelings, and "events" that occur in prayer, and aim at a constant inner silence. The risk here is of quenching the Spirit (1 Thess 5:19), and putting both the disciple and God into a straitjacket where nothing can happen that is not pre-approved by whoever devised the prayer method.

If we turn to the gospels, we see that Jesus maintained a balance between the two ways. On the one hand, he cautioned his followers not to get too excited by their new supernatural powers, but to focus on the more important fact that their names were written in heaven (Luke 10:20). On the other hand, when the Pharisees tried to suppress the hosannas, Jesus re-torted that if his disciples kept silence, the stones themselves would cry out (Luke 19:39-40). Jesus disliked being pressed to perform crowd-pleasing signs and wonders, yet in his trans-figuration, the raising of Lazarus, and numerous other miracles, he did show the people his glory when he judged that the moment was right.

Jesus steered a perfect course between extremes, but we are not perfect, and so we tilt one way or the other, drawing strength from the side we favor but suffering its weaknesses as well. Comparing two imperfect but spiritually advanced people like Francis of Assisi and John of the Cross helps us past the impasse in two ways. First, it shows us that when we get past surface appearances and examine their images more closely, we see that each picture contains both light and dark shades, both daylight and night. Second, the comparison reveals the common passion underlying each saint's unique spiritual style. Both of these men, and indeed all the great masters of prayer through the ages, were passionately in love with God. They experienced that passion as a desire for God, a devastating energy that sheared away all secondary passions and drew every part of their being to a point aimed directly at God. And in that single-minded longing, they willingly embraced any suffering that would draw them closer to their goal, including and especially the pain of the unfulfilled desire itself. To have one's whole being shaped by a desire that can only be fully satisfied after death is, as countless mystics have testified through the ages, the sweetest suffering of all.

Yet most of us aren't being taught this, and as a result, both in our corporate life in the church and in our individual prayer, we fail to fully embrace either the darkness or the light. Not appreciating the role of desire, our relationship to God is distant and tepid; not understanding the role of suffering, we are be-wildered when we find ourselves in darkness. The modest aim of this book is to bring both these aspects of passion together, and show that, whatever it feels like, God's purpose in drawing us into the dark is always love. A lot of people, much smarter and far holier than I, have addressed these matters before now.

But if you're as intimidated by them as I am, perhaps a little book for beginners will be helpful to you. And even if you number the likes of John of the Cross among your best friends, and words like "apophatic" and "kataphatic" are always flying off your tongue, sometimes it helps to hear familiar ideas put in new ways.

Much of what I have to say about passion will draw from the tradition of nuptial mysticism, which has a long history within Christianity. Indeed, it actually predates Christianity, having been established in Judaism with the inclusion of the Song of Songs (Song of Solomon) in the canon of Scripture. It is also found in Islam, particularly within the Sufi tradition. "Nuptial" or "love" mysticism is that prayer in which God or Christ is seen as the divine Bridegroom, and the people of God, corporately and especially individually, are seen as the bride. The emphasis here is on intimacy, which is greatly desired by both parties, and the goal of the relationship is full union. What is striking in love mysticism is the *mutuality* between lovers. Many Christians know they want to draw closer to God, but we are slow to believe that God desires to be one with us—desires it with a greater intensity than we can imagine, an intensity that made the cross worthwhile.

It must be acknowledged at the outset, however, that this imagery does not resonate with some people. There are those who are uncomfortable with the use of romantic metaphors in a spiritual context because they're unacquainted with the tradition, and the whole idea seems alien and disturbing. Others worry that to speak of God as Bridegroom or Lover is to deny God's justice, sovereignty, and holiness, as well as our own sinfulness. This kind of Christian (and it is usually Christians who worry about this) likely finds mysticism itself dodgy enough, but sees love mysticism in particular as a sappy, "Jesus-is-my-boyfriend" sentimentalism, the Christian life as Hallmark card, with nary a cross in sight.

I will be taking up a lot of these objections in the chapters that follow, but allow me three responses right up front. First, to those who just find the whole idea of a passionate God pretty weird: before dismissing the idea, it's worth considering how consistently this imagery has been used through the millennia and across religious traditions to describe the soul's relationship to God. Second, for those who worry that to speak of God's love is to neglect his justice and abhorrence of sin, remember the story of the blind men describing an elephant.[3] We are all blind when it comes to God, and no finite being can fully describe an infinite God in all his (/her) attributes. To focus on God as divine Bridegroom in these pages is not to deny that other imagery—father, mother, brother, friend, king, good shepherd, and yes, final judge—has its place too.

Finally, anyone who sees the intimacy and union with God portrayed in nuptial mysticism as sentimental devotional fluff is not taking the metaphor seriously. The invitation is to a love relationship that will demand everything from us. Scripture teaches us over and over that you cannot draw near to God without being changed. When we consent to that change, the course it will take is out of our hands, but we can be sure that the cross Jesus called us to carry will make its appearance in due time. Those who have accepted the Bridegroom's invitation tend to embrace suffering with a willingness that baffles most people. The cross is indeed central to this way; it was God's passionate love for humankind that brought Jesus to the cross, and when we are ignited with that same passion, we will want to be there with him. In this we see that suffering and desire really do represent two aspects of the same thing, two faces of passion.

Discomfort with highly affective prayer in any form also sometimes arises among those who are committed to a more austere method of prayer, which I alluded to above. This approach emphasizes silence and de-emphasizes thoughts, feelings, and all other "events" that might occur during one's prayer. Centering prayer is a popular example of this type of prayer in our day, but the general school of thought from which centering prayer was developed is many centuries old. Because centering prayer is the focus of a movement that has produced a lot of resources, in the pages that follow I will spend correspondingly more time developing the affective alternative—that is, prayer that is emotionally lush and "event-full."

But the premise of this book is that both forms of prayer are legitimate ways through which the soul draws near to God. Being dogmatic about one or the other is counterproductive, given that a person's prayer "style" is largely a matter of temperament, as well as vocation. God calls each of us to a certain path, and the best possible prayer for each of us is that to which we are called. Emotional highs are not the only mark of passionate prayer, and dwelling in silence is not the sole mark of spiritual maturity. Schools of prayer have a regrettable tendency to become like denominations; it is the aim of this book to advocate a bit of ecumenism.

One final note, on language. I know that there are those who dislike the use of the masculine pronoun with reference to God, and they have good reasons: the first and third Persons of the Trinity do not, after all, have a gender, and to speak of God as "he" is limiting. It reinforces the tendency to see God as the bearded old white guy in the sky, or to identify God with fathers who were well short of divine. On the other hand, to many people the alternatives are awkward and distracting: "God wants to draw all of God's people to Godself" is the kind of sentence that can cause some readers to put a book down forever. There is no pleasing everyone on this one, so my choice is to go with the masculine pronoun, recognizing its limitations, and with apologies to those who wish I'd chosen otherwise.

There are a lot of books out there that try to make sense of suffering. And there are a number of books that speak of how deeply our souls long for God. In this book, I want to show that these are not two separate things that may or may not be a part of a person's spiritual journey. Suffering and desire are inextricably linked; they are like the dark and bright sides of one moon. And although each individual will have unique experiences of each, both are central to the life of faith. The same

One who called us to carry our cross also called us to love him with all our heart, soul, mind, and strength.

These are the two faces of passion, and in the chapters that follow, we will explore them both. I confess I find the prospect of writing on such huge subjects more than a bit daunting. But as a Third Order Franciscan, I am bound by a Rule that contains the following:

> When asked to undertake work of which we feel unworthy or incapable, we do not shrink from it on the grounds of humility, but confidently attempt it through the power that is made perfect in weakness. (*The Principles of the Third Order*, Day Twenty Four)

If anything useful emerges in these pages, you can be sure that God is showing off, proving his power through my weakness. This is not a concert, performed by a master musician. Think of it more as karaoke. With that understood, let us begin.

Chapter One

The Two Faces of Passion

> The poetry of passionate love is the accurate language of theology.
>
> —Rosemary Haughton, *The Passionate God*

Among my closest friends are two lifelong Christians, women of deep faith. Both are struggling with that faith at the moment: one is weary with the endless drama of a dysfunctional family, and while she's not about to lose her faith, her practice has become hollow and perfunctory of late. The other has entered a period of spiritual darkness; a series of losses and transitions have left her disoriented in a world God seems to have fled.

My friends are not alone in their struggles. Boredom afflicts many of us, either because we've lost the excitement that first brought us to Jesus, or because we never knew it to begin with. Our religious routines seem such a long way from the zeal that carried our spiritual forebears to the stake, the gas chamber, or wherever else they were pleased to throw away their lives for the love of God. And all suffering—including spiritual suffering—is capable of leaving us lost and bewildered: we don't know how to cope with our own pain, or respond to the pain of others. We can't explain why a loving God allows life to break

1

our hearts, and seems so far away just when we most need to feel the reassurance of the divine presence.

The mystery at the heart of both these problems, and the life of faith itself, is *passion*. Every person who responds to the call of Christ is cast into a passion play, given a part in a story of love too big and too powerful for mortals to control. This is not the passion of chick flicks and bodice-rippers, passion as Hollywood understands it. To begin to grasp the passion at the heart of the Christian story, we need older and wiser teachers.

"Passion" is one of those strange words—like "sanction"—that has two distinct and seemingly opposite meanings. It has both positive and negative connotations: strong desire, on the one hand, and suffering, on the other. The mystics and troubadours of medieval Europe understood this well, and they could not conceive of a love that didn't include both faces of passion. In the tradition of courtly love, the romantic ideal was the knight pledged to a worthy lady (who was, very likely, married to someone else; this does not seem to have been regarded as a problem). In the service of his lady, the knight would expect to endure heroic ordeals. No notion of "cheap grace" here, only total fidelity through every trial, fueled by a complete capitulation to the beauty and virtue of the lady. A love unwilling to suffer was not worthy of the name; real love gives the costliest gifts, and counts it an honor to empty its purse for the sake of the beloved.

The troubadours entertained at court with songs of heroic love, but the genius of the medieval mystics was to turn this romantic ideal in the direction of the soul's relationship to God. Francis of Assisi, and Beguines[1] such as Mechthild of Magdeburg and Hadewijch of Brabant, to name just a few, understood themselves to be engaged in a spiritual quest that was passionate in both senses. Francis betrothed himself to Lady Poverty, the constant companion of Christ on earth, and so close to Jesus that in Francis's writings it is often difficult to tell them apart. The writing of the Beguines also includes a playful gender-bending in their conception of God: Christ is the Lover who appears in his full humanity, including his full masculinity, while the Trinity is conceived as the noble Lady, called *Minne* or "Love." In their writings and their lives, all these mystics embraced suffering as part of the bargain, and their ardor never flagged though they all knew times of great darkness. Here is Hadewijch:

> The ways of Love are strange,
>   As those who have followed them well know,
>   For, unexpectedly, She withdraws Her consolation.
>   He whom Love touches
>   Can enjoy no stability
>   And he will taste
>   Many a nameless hour.[2]

What is so compelling about all these lovers of God is that they never fell victim to the twin illusions that life is boring and that suffering is meaningless. Possessing the romantic imagination, they understood themselves as small people with a great call. Everyday decisions can seem trivial to us, because the spiritual realm is veiled by the world of the senses. But as Jesus observed, tiny seeds can have surprisingly large consequences. The Middle Ages were a kind of golden age of mysticism, and produced lovers of God who knew both suffering and desire to the fullest, to the point where they become indistinguishable. Their work is finding renewed appreciation in our day, and will be cited often in the pages to follow. If these mystics, along with their spiritual descendants in our day, can bring the two faces of passion into sharper focus for us, perhaps we will begin to see our way to a deeper intimacy with this passionate God.

Passion as Desire

William James said that religion exists in some as an acute fever, in others as a dull habit. In the revelation to St. John on Patmos,

we hear Jesus moving between sadness and anger at the bland-
ness and boredom of some of his earliest followers. His call to the
church at Ephesus is wistful: "You have walked away from your
first love—why?" (Rev 2:4 MSG). To the church at Laodicea,
he is more stern: "You're not cold, you're not hot—far better
to be either cold or hot! You're stale. You're stagnant. You make
me want to vomit" (Rev 3:15 MSG).

The idea of nauseating Jesus is pretty scary, but we haven't
really changed. I once heard Rowan Williams, the archbishop
of Canterbury, say that if we Christians are not attracting people
to Christ, it's because when we look at him, we don't seem to
be seeing anything very special. This was not true of Francis or
the Beguines, because as mystics, they saw God with unusual
clarity. (I would add that prophets are those who see the world
with unusual clarity. Both are given these gifts so they can help
the rest of us see better.) When they looked at Christ, what they
saw changed everything, because that look was what Charles
Williams called the "Beatrician moment," "the one when a
person breaks through to a wholly other sphere of experience,
and the eyes of the lover are both dazzled and endowed with
new vision."[3]

That moment is transformative; it casts a halo around everything, making the world sweeter and the one we love unrecog-
nizably beautiful. We joke that love is blind, but perhaps it is
lovers alone who see truly, past the flaws to the person the
beloved was meant to be, and will be when Christ has made all
things new. But for the one who looks at Christ himself, seeing
clearly, there are only two responses possible: desire or rejection.
So perhaps what we really need to overcome our spiritual apathy
is to spend more time simply looking at him. As the peasant
told the Curate of Ars, the simplest prayer can be the most
profound: "I look at him, and he looks at me."

When Francis of Assisi looked at Christ, he tended to babble,
as lovers often do:

May the power of your love, Lord Christ, fiery and sweet as honey, wean my heart from all that is under heaven, so that I may die for love of your love, who were so good as to die for love of my love. Amen.[4]

Being something of a poet, Francis babbled more beautifully than most. But it was an early follower of Francis, Jacopone of Todi (d. 1306), whose poetry really captured the intensity of this love. In one of Jacopone's famous *Lauds*, Christ speaks to the beloved soul:

> My bride, the wonder of this exchange of love!
> When you beseech Me, you command Me;
> Love makes Me suffer, drives Me mad,
> Drawing Me outside of Myself and closer to you.
> Delay no longer, My bride, yield to Me, take Me,
> As I give Myself to you, and give Me your heart.
>
> Yield to Me, My desire, My love;
> Be one with Me, bride of My heart.
> Satisfy My longing, come and be My spouse.
> Caught on the hook of Love, I yearn for you.
> That is why I call to you, My bride, embrace you chastely,
> Come down to you in the ardor of My love.[5]

When Jacopone looked at Christ, what he saw set his soul alight. This should not surprise us, since Scripture tells us that God is love (1 John 4:8), and that God is a consuming fire (Heb 12:29). A consuming fire of love, infinite, all powerful, all knowing but still loving with a consuming, raging love—well, we've been warned. The incarnation occurred precisely because God desired to touch and embrace and possess the most sacred, most intimate part of us. If we're bored in the presence of such a love, we are clearly not paying attention. Where is the way back to our first love? It is right before us: "I look at him, and he looks at me."

The Language of Desire

The language of medieval love mysticism can, as I have noted, sound alien and disturbing, even shocking, to modern ears. The Franciscan writer John Michael Talbot has observed as much:

> Many of my friends are shocked the first time they hear prayer being described in romantic terms. For them, there's something improper or even slightly sacrilegious about comparing prayer, a thing so lofty and spiritual, to love. But it didn't bother Francis or other saints. They could think of no better way to describe the union between God and humans.[6]

How can it be appropriate to speak of one's relationship to God in these terms? Isn't there something a little sleazy about applying romantic, even erotic, language to what is holy? It's a fair question, and at this point I have three answers, or perhaps three beginnings of answers, which I will elaborate more fully as we go.

First, as Dorothee Soelle has pointed out, there is no getting around the simple linguistic observation that, through the ages, mystics *have* used such language to express the inexpressible.[7] That those who have known God most intimately have regularly—across time and across cultures—resorted to the language of romantic love to speak of that knowing, is in itself suggestive. In the effort to describe mystical experience, language falters and fails us. So, we may give up on language altogether, and declare that God, and all his dealings with us, are beyond language, beyond images and concepts. There is, as I have mentioned, a long history of this approach in mystical literature.

If we don't give up on language, though, we'll find it necessary to reach for images, analogies, metaphors that express desire in ways most people can recognize. We'll see that there are multiple vocabularies of desire, and teachers of prayer have made use of them all. But most of them eventually fall back on the language of romantic love, simply because it is the human vocabulary that's oriented to intense desire. There is a technical language of mysticism that speaks of "recollection," the "prayer of quiet," "transforming union," and the like. But this is the language of salivary glands and digestive enzymes, which can't begin to capture the experience of a ripe peach whose nectar runs down your arms. Erotic language is an attempt to convey that kind of experience.

Second, I want to emphasize that when we speak of eros in this context, we are not concerned primarily with sexuality; it's not about genitalia. Ronald Rolheiser describes eros as "an unquenchable fire, a restlessness, a longing, a disquiet, a hunger, a loneliness, a gnawing nostalgia, a wildness that cannot be tamed, a congenital all-embracing ache that lies at the center of human experience and is the ultimate force that drives every-thing else."[8] Sexual attraction is only one manifestation of eros; more fundamentally, eros is a force, a kind of energy. It's the energy that produces babies, to be sure, but it also produces great art, breakthroughs in science, and tireless campaigns for social justice. My sister is a chef, and one of the reasons she's successful is that she's passionate about food. She's fascinated by ingredients, spends her time thinking of new ways to use them, and works with attentiveness and precision because she will give it nothing short of her best. This drive to create in the medium of food is an expression of eros in her life. In another person's life it might be the drive to rescue abandoned pets. Eros is simply the flame within us, and it can be used to light all kinds of fires.

It follows, then, and this is the third point, that while many mystics have described their experience in the language of romantic love, this language will not resonate with everyone. There are other images to use, however; we will be looking also at the language of nostalgia, of exile—the longing for home, where the "home" is in God. We'll also examine the language of the desert: Jesus was "driven" by the Spirit into the desert at a crucial moment in his life, and we too find ourselves driven, or perhaps drawn, there at times as well. Whether we go out there to wrestle with the demons or with God, it's that same divine restlessness that compels us to go.

There are all kinds of vocabularies people use to talk about their encounters with God. We can learn a lot about our connection to the divine by thinking of God as Father or Mother, of Jesus as brother or friend, or of God as a deep, unknowable mystery. All of these are useful, and probably all of them are easier to swallow, and therefore more commonly heard in our day, than the language of romantic love. Although I consider various kinds of imagery in this book, I pay special attention to romantic imagery, both because it's less familiar and makes us uncomfortable, and because it conveys aspects of the relationship that aren't captured by other imagery, especially the intensity with which God loves us.

There are limitations to this imagery, and we'll consider those too. But as spiritual writers have found for thousands of years, and are rediscovering in our day, God does desire us passionately. For some that feels awkward, even distasteful. But for those who are called to this particular path to God, it is the invitation to a great adventure.

Passion as Suffering

The God who loves us passionately sets our souls alight, but also leads us through the valley of shadows. Though we typically associate passion with the pleasant feeling of ardent desire, we do well to remind ourselves that the Latin root of the word *passion* means *suffering*. The church reminds us of this once a year in Holy Week, when we turn our attention to our Lord's Passion. And the church does teach us how to deal with many kinds of suffering: to respond generously to the needs of others, to be steadfast in the face of persecution, to regret our sins and endure with patience and trust both the irritations and tragedies of ordinary life.

But there are two kinds of suffering for which the church does not prepare us very well: spiritual darkness, and the fact that love hurts, and loving God can hurt a lot. It's not for want of resources—we have the theology, practical wisdom, and exemplars in abundance, but they're not routinely shared with ordinary laypeople. The result is that we meet these experiences unprepared, and struggle to make sense of them. Not succeeding, many of us give up and leave, unnecessary casualties in a war fought with half our ammunition still in the box it came in.

The mystics who have had the most powerful experiences of God's presence also knew dark and arid times when God seemed absent. Nighttime in the desert offers few comforts, and its consolations are an acquired taste. Intellectually, we know that God is never truly absent, yet this knowledge did not stop Jesus from crying out, *Why have you forsaken me?* Taking up the cross means sharing that experience too, yet many of us are taken by surprise when the light goes dim and we feel the sand in our teeth.

So we search for explanations. Maybe I've sinned. Maybe I'm not trying hard enough. God is losing patience, is bored, has moved on. Maybe I'm not on God's A-list. The party is somewhere else, and I'm not invited. I'm abandoned, and cry with the psalmist:

> God, God . . . my God!
> Why did you dump me miles from nowhere?
> Doubled up with pain, I call to God
>   all the day long. No answer. Nothing. (Ps 22:1-2 MSG)

It's so easy to assume or assign blame when God goes into hiding—I've failed God, or God has failed me—if we haven't been schooled in the divine style of courtship. It's a kind of dance, and when God steps back from us, it's to draw us in closer. God pulls us into the dark, not to leave us but to bring us into deeper intimacy; after all, intimate things go on in the dark. In his exploration of the dark night of the soul, John of the Cross shows that the experience of spiritual darkness is a very special call, and in that darkness God performs a special loving work in the soul of the beloved. Long before John wrote, however, the medieval mystics testified to the importance of this kind of suffering for the soul's maturation:

> The ultimate mystic experience is for [Hadewijch] the recognition that God is most intimately present at the moment when he seems most absent . . . her sense of the absence of God and the desire for his presence caused her real psychological suffering. She learned that it is within the sense of God's absence that union takes place.[9]

Again and again the Beguines cried out their agony when God withdrew. Listen to Mechthild:

> How painfully I long for you . . .
> For I suffer inhuman anguish.
> Human death I would find more pleasant . . .
> I seek you with my thoughts
> As a maiden secretly does her lover . . .
> I cry out to you in great longing,
> A lonely voice;
> I hope for your coming with heavy heart,
> I cannot rest, I am on fire,
> Unquenchable in your burning love.[10]

She concludes: "Whoever becomes entangled in longing such as this must forever hang blessedly fettered in God."[11] Finally, Mechthild draws together the threads of intimate love and suffering:

> Lord, what shall we now say of love?
> Now that we lie so close on the bed of my pain.[12]

These mystics are not talking about seeking out suffering for the sake of holiness, though extreme acts of penitence were common enough at the time. The suffering they describe was the result of God's seeming withdrawal, and the ensuing sense of darkness and emptiness. What made their experience of spiritual darkness endurable was that they understood what God was up to:

> The message of Hadewijch's mystic theology is that it is at the moment of feeling lost in the dark, of feeling crushed by despair, that (wo)man comes closest to being one with the God-Man. Hadewijch learns that it is only in the suffering caused by the absence of love that desire becomes so great as to become one with that love.[13]

How much more hopefully we could bear up under this pain if we understood it in positive terms. All pilgrims need to know that the longer one journeys toward Christ, the more likely the path will take a turn through dark places, and that finding ourselves in the dark is a sign of favor, not failure. And a sign of closeness: sometimes I cannot see Christ, or much of anything, because my face is buried in his chest. He fills my entire field of vision, and I can't see him, not because he's so far away but because he's so near.

Yet even the presence of God can cause suffering. Love hurts—love *itself* hurts—and love for an infinite God can hurt almost beyond human endurance: "The Beatrician experience is *painful*. Even in its joy it has a quality of longing"[14] because of our human incapacity for complete union. We simply cannot close the gap: "That hurts, with a sense of ineffable 'wrongness,' yet that 'wrongness' is the indication of something so 'right' that to be rid of the hurt would be unthinkably worse than bearing it."[15] This is why so many mystics have welcomed suffering in a way that seems almost masochistic: they understand that pain to be the price of a desire that cannot be fully satisfied in this life. But having tasted something of the sweetness, they would not return to a bland existence, even for the sake of peace.

Sweetness, darkness, emptiness, and desire—our medieval teachers knew both faces of passion intimately. The journey has its quiet moments too; any great quest includes periods of waiting. But if we understand that we wait on a passionate God who does some very fine work in the dark, we will wait in hope, not in boredom or despair.

Part I

Desire

Chapter Two

The Good News, Part Two

The most difficult thing in mature believing is to accept
that I am an object of God's delight.

—Alan Jones, *Exploring Spiritual Direction*

If you did a survey of Christians that asked the question,
"What is the 'good news'?" you'd get quite a wide variety of
answers that reflect both differences in personal understanding
and different traditions within the church. There are those who
would advise you that although you're lost in your sin and have
dug yourself into a debt you can never repay, the good news is
that Jesus paid the debt with his death, and if you'll confess your
sin and ask him for forgiveness, you'll be saved. Others would
speak of the incarnation of God in Christ, of God's presence in
the world as a being at once human and divine, rendering the
world and all that's in it sacred, redeemed, holy. If you could get
these people together, you might be treated to a lively debate
on the atonement; if so, you should make some popcorn and
settle in for the evening. I once had a dream in which I was
invited to a friend's family party, where everyone had brought
a different type of brownies—one for every theory of the atonement. The ones I tried were the "penal substitutionary atonement

brownies," which were so sinful and deadly that you'd better let Jesus eat them for you.

The South African theologian Albert Nolan has said that the "good news" must be connected specifically to every time and place.[1] There is a universal, "generic" gospel, if you will, but unless people see it as an answer to questions they're actually asking, it won't be perceived as good news. In the context of South Africa under apartheid, for example, the good news was that all humans have equal beauty, dignity, and worth in the sight of God, and that the judgments of man and his oppressive systems are not the final word. That's certainly good news for those who are marginalized in our time and place as well, but there's plenty of good news for middle-class white folks like myself too. For us, it's good news indeed that our worth before God is not dependent on being rich and famous, young and beautiful, successful and strong. And it's especially good news that even the lives we've screwed up, seemingly beyond repair, can be resurrected and transformed. Our mistakes, failures, and addictions; our enslavement to our own egos and our selfish disregard for others; our frenzied inattentiveness to what's important, and consequent failure to actually live the lives we've been given—all of these rags and tatters can be rescued from the sewing room floor, and incorporated into a garment that will astonish us one day with its beauty and the perfection of its fit.

While they would have different ways of putting it, and different theological concepts for explaining it, virtually all Christians would recognize this as a version of the "good news." But lately I've been wondering if there isn't a "good news beyond the good news," a "good news, part two," perhaps, the part that many Christians still need to hear. One way or another, all Christians understand that God loved us enough to rescue us, but I wonder how many of us really have any idea of the magnitude of that love, or the implications of it. I know that for many years, I figured God loved me as a generic unit of humanity: one member of a race he'd committed himself to doing something about, one more fallen chessman to put back in its square on the board. If God included me in the plan for humankind's redemption, it was really out of an aesthetic that doesn't tolerate loose ends. God is like an efficient housewife, who sees no point in loading the dishwasher if you're going to leave crumbs all over the counter. I was one of those crumbs lurking under the toaster, and in her infinite thoroughness, she was going to bin me in the end.

Wouldn't it be interesting to have a museum with a gallery of the false images of God we humans have constructed over the years? My "God as Housewife" idol could be in there with the Angry Judge, the Abusive Father Who Killed His Own Son, the Dotty Old Man in the Sky, the Cosmic Santa, and all the rest. I do think that one of the most popular and enduring of these is the various versions of the distant God who is willing to rescue us units of humanity, but once he's ticked that off his to-do list, he's ready to move on to something else. If we Christians stay with this image of God, it's because we haven't heard part two of the good news, which is this: there's a reason for the ancient tradition that a human being cannot see the face of God and live. The reason is that God is much bigger, much *more*, than any of our ideas about him. And this bigger, "more" God is passionately in love with every human soul, including even yours and mine.

Let's think about this a bit. While acknowledging the limitations of all our images of God, there is one that I find more helpful and less misleading than most. Spend a moment calling to mind the things we humans really admire, our highest values. What would be on your list? I admire the strength of those who protect the weak; the sacrificial dedication of those who live their lives in the service of their children, their neighbors, or their God. I admire the ability to create beauty, whether in paint, music, architecture, poetry, or prose. I admire the kind of intellect that can put complicated ideas in simple, comprehensible form without oversimplifying them. And I admire the wisdom that is able to tune out seductive distractions, and stay focused on what really matters. You will have your own list, but there will be much overlap, many things we all agree are beautiful, noble, inspired.

Now imagine that each of these is a little spark in the night, coming up from behind us and flying past in an arc of light. We admire each one as it flies over our shoulder, blazing briefly and then disappearing into the distance. "Mother Teresa: cool!" "Brahms's Requiem: brilliant!" "String theory: fascinating!" But while we appreciate these flickering lights as they pass us, what we don't see is that each of them is actually a spark off a great, roaring bonfire at our back, and that bonfire is God.[2] God is the source of all nobility of spirit, all beauty, all wisdom. God is the creative genius who invented creative genius, the love that is the source of all loves, the passion from which all passions come, and where, ultimately, they all lead. And this very God, this incomprehensible mystery, this blazing, roaring bonfire of love, so powerful that the unmediated sight of it would reduce us to ashes—this God loves me more than I even want to be loved.

This is good news indeed, and to be honest, it's taken me years to believe it. If we take it seriously, really sit with it long enough to take it in, it seems too good to be true. The psalmist who proclaimed the excellence of God and then wrote, "What is man, that thou art mindful of him? and the son of man, that thou visitest him?" (Ps 8:4), had obviously reached the same conclusion: too good to be true. But God is ultimate goodness, and perfect truth; therefore, that which is most good is most true. That God loves us this much is precisely what Jesus was trying to get across in his stories of the shepherd hunting down the lone lost sheep, the housewife sweeping the whole house in search of one lost coin, the father of the prodigal son (Luke 15). When that housewife found the coin, she gave a party—it probably cost her more than the coin was worth. God is nutty like that, because love does make you a little crazy. The prodigal son had not only left his father but massively insulted him on the way out, by asking for his inheritance, thereby saying he wished his father dead. Yet this ill-used father completely abandoned his dignity the moment he spotted his son in the distance, and *ran* to meet him, a thing fathers in that culture did not do.

What Jesus is trying to tell us in these stories is that the God who invented beauty, who spoke into existence a world meeting the complex and wildly improbable conditions that would permit the development of life, who designed the ingenious system that creates human life out of love and pleasure—this God seeks every human soul with a desire that will pay any price to be one with us, including his own human life, voluntarily taken, and voluntarily laid down. And he seeks each of us individually, not as generic units of humanity. I once saw a movie in which a young nun was dressed as a bride for the occasion of taking her vows. To the woman who was helping her dress, she spoke her joy about being the bride of Christ. "Well," said the other woman, "he's got an awful lot of brides, hasn't he?" The nun replied, "Yes, but he loves me as if I'm the only one." The good news is not only that Jesus died for us all, but that he would have died for me even if I'd been the only one. The shepherd had other sheep; the housewife had other coins; the father had another son. But it didn't make any difference, because when a single one was lost, there would be no rest until it was restored.

Christians talk a lot about salvation, but I wonder if we really consider what we mean by it? I imagine that for many people, the word "salvation" conjures up an image of tent revivals, of pleas to "come to Jesus" backed by cringeworthy music, of being interrogated about whether one has gotten "right with God." "Salvation" implies being saved *from* something, so we might think of being saved from the fires of hell, and imagine that salvation feels like that big adrenaline hit you get when you've had a near-miss at sixty-five on the freeway. Some people dismiss salvation as floating on clouds playing harps all day, in the company of prissy do-gooders and smug saints in shiny robes. You'd have to be crazy to want to be saved for that, and I agree that a hell full of interesting sinners sounds much more fun.

But as C. S. Lewis once said, if you can't understand books for grown-ups, you shouldn't try to talk about them. These childish images don't get us very close to salvation as it's portrayed in the Bible and by the mystics who've seen God with some clarity. Let's begin with Jesus' first words to his disciples when he appeared to them in his resurrected glory: Shalom—"Peace be with you" (John 20:19). The Hebrew word "shalom" means "peace," but this peace is much bigger, much richer than just the absence of conflict. Shalom means a state of total well-being, of physical, emotional, spiritual, intellectual, and material wholeness.

Let's try a little thought experiment here. Take a few moments to imagine yourself whole, healed completely in every way, in every dimension of your life. I don't mean imagine your wounds scarred over; that's fixing, not healing. Imagine your wounds as if they never existed. The kid who bullied you on the playground, the moments you've felt embarrassed or ashamed, the dysfunctional relationships you've endured, the illnesses and injuries, the addictions, the sins that have boomeranged back on you and bruised your own soul. Imagine that you were never discriminated against, never made to feel insignificant, never had to rage at injustice. In short, imagine you'd never hurt or been hurt. You'd be like a child, you'd be back in the Garden, naked and unashamed.

But wait—there's more! The "shalom" God wishes for us is not just the absence of trauma; it cannot be defined only in negative terms. God's intention is that we participate in Christ's resurrection, and share in his glory, and his joy.[3] To become "Christlike" (Phil 2:5) is more than just avoiding all the big sins and small vices that Jesus avoided. Think about *who Jesus really is.* In his transfiguration, he showed his closest friends a glimpse of his true identity, and they fell on their faces, overcome with awe. "His face did shine as the sun, and his garments became white as the light" (Matt 17:2 ASV).

Salvation means that this light-filled Being calls us to himself, and that in his embrace we too are suffused with light, filled with a joy and completeness, a rightness and wholeness we can feel in our blood and bones. Among Jesus' last words to his disciples before his Passion were promises that he would give to them his own peace, his own joy.[4] The God who created peace, joy, awe, happiness, and fun promises to fill our cup till it overflows. The salvation Jesus gives us surpasses every fleeting human pleasure (yes, *all* of them). And the good news is that, although complete fulfillment of these promises awaits our own resurrection, the life "in Christ" St. Paul loved to speak of is not something we can know only after death. It begins here and now.

So if that's the good news, what do we do with it? I think the first thing to do is to just sit and be stunned by it. This is the kind of truth about the faith that one can repeat as a new convert, but I've come to believe that it takes years of serious attention for it to travel the eighteen or so inches from the brain to the heart. What about the foot-long journey back to the mouth? Good news is, after all, intended to be told. It's at this point that most of us go into the cold sweat reliably generated by the word "evangelism." I've heard Christians lament our gutlessness about spreading the faith, arguing that if we learned of a cure for AIDS or even saved a bundle on our car insurance, we wouldn't hesitate to tell everyone the good news. But that complaint overlooks the fact that being cornered by a proselytizing Christian comes just after public speaking on most people's dread list. It's easy to see why St. Francis's advice to "preach the gospel at all times, and use words if necessary" is so popular: most of us don't want to use words, and probably won't even if it is necessary. I include myself in this camp. And so we feel a vague sense of unease whenever someone uses the E-word, feeling that somehow we're responsible for this evangelism thing, but without a clue what to do about it.

I think the reason evangelism is such a scary idea to most people, both victims and perpetrators, or would-be perps, is that it's so often been fueled by an incomplete understanding of the good news itself. When someone sneaks up and brains you with the gospel, subjecting you to a glassy-eyed recitation of the four spiritual laws and inviting you to swallow redemption like a pill, that person has not heard part two of the good news. When we've really seen something of God, turned around and gazed at the beauty of the bonfire, seen its light and felt its heat, we will not be able to mouth facile formulas; indeed, we may not be able to speak at all. Not for nothing has mystic experience been classically described as "ineffable," indescribable, beyond words. The deepest experiences of God often occur in silence, beyond silence, even.[5]

And yet, as Kieran Kavanaugh has observed, mystics tend to have "an irrepressible urge toward some kind of outward expression of their experiences of God, at least of the more intense ones."[6] As someone has said, we keep trying to "eff" the ineffable. What do we do with the dilemma of longing to communicate what is beyond words? Jesus warned us that even pearls, cast to the wrong audience at the wrong moment, are only going to get us mauled for our pains (Matt 7:6).

Perhaps we wear the intensity of our love next to our skin, like a slip. Sometimes the slip slips, dips below the hemline, and someone catches a glimpse of lace. Perhaps lace is the good news, that little bit of finery people will spot from time to time if they're watching us at all closely. Maybe we don't need to open a trench coat and terrify people with the gospel, and maybe the fact that some Christians keep trying to do so accounts for the trauma many people associate with being an evangelistic target. As Albert Nolan suggests, it's not good news if it doesn't answer questions we're actually asking. Part one of the good news tells us that Jesus has defeated our twin enemies, sin and death. In our culture, some people feel a crippling sense of guilt, and some don't; for those who don't, hearing that "sin" has been defeated may not even be intelligible, much less good news. But there's no variation in the degree to which we're threatened by death, though we do vary in our willingness to admit it. If death has been redefined as the threshold of new life or, to put it in less individualistic terms, as admission to the party of all parties where the truly beautiful people hang out, that is certainly good news. And it's reason enough for many of us to embrace the Christian faith.

But if we stop there, we are not fully embracing the faith— more like politely shaking hands with it. Signing on for salvation is something like entering a contractual relationship: a covenant, as we say. But part two of the good news is that this magnificent and passionate God, the God who is always, eternally, and incomprehensibly *more*, is inviting us into a love affair. When we think the news is too good to be true, we're like someone standing under Niagara Falls with a teacup, worrying that it won't be enough. Our real concern should be how to trade our teacup for a bucket, so we can hold a little more of this inexhaustible supply of love.

One of the great human dilemmas is that many of us have both a horror of anonymity on the one hand, and on the other, a firm conviction that we would not be loved if we were fully known. This is exactly why we spend so much time, money, and energy trying to manipulate how others see us, disguising our faces and figures, our motives and neuroses, lest people reject us once they figure out how unlovable we really are. If you don't believe we fear this, go into any drugstore, head for the "feminine hygiene" aisle, and consider the array of products whose message is, "the most intimate part of your body is unpleasant and must be disguised." And although women have been hammered particularly hard with this, men have their own versions. What part two of the gospel says is this: the Source of all beauty knows everything about us, and desires us *as ourselves*—not in spite of who we are, but because of who we are. He knows that parts of us aren't pretty. We may be surprised to find out which parts those are. But the more I come to know him, the more I realize that it's not a disguised, sanitized, tarted-up version of me he wants. He asks me to offer him my true self, so that he can give me back my truest self, the one he created to be his in love forever. To be so loved, by such a God—it turns out that it is the best news that's most true after all.

Chapter Three

Pyrophobia:
In Fear of the Flame

Is it not the case that, in some sense, a life devoid of passion, like a life devoid of reflection, is a life not worth living?

—Elizabeth A. Dreyer, *Passionate Spirituality:*
Hildegard of Bingen and Hadewijch of Brabant

Jesus Christ came into the world as the incarnate Word of God. This statement is the kind of insider church-speak that would have sent me screaming from the room in the days when I was tentatively reconsidering the Christian faith—if I hadn't fallen asleep first. It's a bit like saying that chocolate is "a number of raw and processed foods that originate from the seed of the tropical cacao tree,"[1] or that caviar is "the processed, salted roe of certain species of fish, most notably the sturgeon."[2] These statements are technically correct, maximally boring, and give no hint of the ecstasy that awaits when the reality hits your tongue. In a similar way, my bit of churchy jargon hides a momentous reality under a blanket of boredom.

When we say that Jesus was and is the incarnate Word of God, we mean something like this: the man Jesus, a human being occupying a fleshly body as all humans do, was God the Father's full and complete expression of himself. To look at Jesus is to see the Father (John 14:9), "[f]or in him the entire fullness of God's nature dwells bodily" (Col 2:9 Holman). Everything the Father has to say about himself, he has said in Jesus, in whom is manifest each of the infinite facets of God. Because Jesus is fully God, we can learn what we want to know about God from him. But because he is also fully human, looking at Jesus can teach us some things about ourselves as well. One thing I learn from looking at him is that we too are meant to manifest facets of God, in our finite, imperfect ways. Rowan Williams has said that if Jesus is the Word of God, then we who share his humanity are also words of God, not divine but made in the divine image.[3] The startling implication of this is that each of us also represents a statement God is making about himself. Each of us is a bit of truth God is speaking to the world, and our purpose in life is to proclaim that truth clearly to a world in need of good news.

Another implication of saying that each individual person conveys some aspect of God is that our uniqueness as individuals, and our diversity as a species, are crucial to God's plan. Our differences of body, mind, and spirit are not inconveniences to be tolerated, but in themselves reveal the lushness of the creative mind of God. This is why the tendency I referred to earlier of some religious teachers to stress one aspect of the spiritual life to the exclusion of others, and push everyone to conform to their methods and expectations, is so disastrously wrong. It's not just oppressive and hurtful; it also reveals a faulty theology that undervalues the richness and underestimates the autonomy of God. This tendency is not new, however, nor is it particularly rare, and one area in which it has been especially damaging is prayer. Through the ages, religious authorities have found it difficult to resist the temptation to try to regulate people's relationships to God. And while various forms of institutional discipline, including violence, have been used toward that end, a more subtle means is to hold up one model or method of prayer as the only acceptable way to God.

There's no telling how much damage this has caused, or how many people this kind of exclusivity has ushered out the church doors. We may be one people in Christ, but we have a lot of little subcultures, and we can get pretty obnoxious about them. There are places in the church where you're expected to wave your hands and sway to the music, and others where such behavior would be greeted with horror. Some assume that liturgical churches where most of the service follows a set script are stuffy and unemotional, while others find in the quiet and lack of distracting novelties an opportunity to sink into awe. I think the different traditions that have evolved within the church are God's way of redeeming our tragic divisions, in that there's something for everyone and most anyone who really wants to can find a corner where they can feel at home. We become tyrannical when we insist that the spiritual style that suits our particular temperament is the only way, and those whose approach is more emotional or more cerebral, more solitary or more community focused, more demonstrative or more reserved, are less authentic in their faith and less acceptable to God.

What's true of spiritual styles overall is doubly true of our approach to prayer, and we see this especially when we focus on contemplative prayer. There, too, we see differences in approach that reflect differences of temperament, as well as the prerogative of God to choose his own means of dealing with the human soul. Traditionally, the two principle forms of mysticism are the apophatic and the kataphatic:

> The apophatic tradition, the *via negativa*, emphasizes the radical difference between God and creatures. God is best reached, therefore, by negation, forgetting, and unknowing, in a darkness of mind without the support of concepts, images, and symbols.

God is not this, not that. Kataphatic mysticism, the *via affirma-tiva*, emphasizes the similarity that exists between God and creatures. Because God can be found in all things, the affirmative way recommends the use of concepts, images, and symbols as a way of contemplating God.[4]

How do these translate into lived contemplative experience? Janet K. Ruffing[5] has captured the difference in a way that is worth quoting at length. The kataphatic path includes the way of "love mysticism":

[It] feels like romantic love: God arouses the desires of the human beloved, engages in courtship, and makes love with the human beloved. The human process of adapting to this reality in the states of awakening, recognition, purification, surrender, and transformation tend to take place through the alternation of felt presence and absence . . .

A second path is more apophatic in its feel. It takes place with fewer reported "events." The quality of experience feels more vague. We yearn for God, who paradoxically feels absent and present simultaneously. This path typically minimizes feeling and emphasizes darkness; prayer usually consists of quiet, silent, loving attention toward God.[6]

We could celebrate these differences, seeing in them a reflection of the rich complexity of God. But we humans, once we've identified categories, seem incapable of resisting the urge to rank them. This is brutally evident in the history of our scientific inquiry into humankind itself: the "age of exploration" brought Europeans into contact with previously unknown populations, and the cognitive step from categories to hierarchies was taken with fatal inevitability. Similarly, as the apophatic and kataphatic approaches to prayer have developed over the ages, church leaders have not been able to resist ranking one over the other. A look at the history of these two traditions of mysticism and the tug-of-war that has taken place over them and over con-templative prayer in general, both in the church and in the larger culture, will give us a context for considering the role of desire in humans' connection to a passionate God.

Greeks and Their Gifts: Cultural Opposition to Passion

Western culture, both secular and religious, has never really been at ease with passion. The roots of our distrust of emotion in general, and intense emotion in particular, reach back at least to ancient Greek philosophy. The Greeks gave us that well-known threefold hierarchy of loves, in which *eros*, or romantic, sexual love, is the lowest; *philia*, or mutual love, is higher; and the highest is *agape*, or selfless, sacrificial love. Eros is the realm of the passions; if not restrained by reason, they will lead to disorder and madness, but reason is capable of detaching the human mind and heart from the passions. This detachment, or *apatheia*, is necessary for the cultivation of agape. As reason is superior to the emotions, and must be their master, so the mind is elevated above the body, and masters it as well. This is bad news for women, who because of their reproductive capacity were linked in the Greek mind with both emotions and the body, while reason and the mind were associated with masculinity.[7]

Hellenistic thought profoundly shaped the Mediterranean world, in which the Jewish religion lived and the Christian faith was born. As a result, both Judaism and Christianity were influenced by Greek ideas, burdened by a legacy of dualism that was foreign to each but seductive to both. The Jewish account of creation, in which God pronounced the world "very good," and the Christian doctrine of the incarnation of God in the person of Jesus both affirm the sacred nature of the material world. But Christian thinking was never consistent in its opposition to Greek dualism, and we haven't gotten over it yet.

It didn't help that an influential figure like the apostle Paul used the word "flesh" to mean at one time the physical body, and at another the unconverted part of us that wars against the spirit. His inconsistent usage made it easy to equate the spirit with "good" and the body with "evil," which is certainly not what he intended. Likewise, Christian writers often used the term "passion" when they were really speaking of *disordered* passions: lust, greed, gluttony, wrath, and the like.[8] As a result, the distinction between licit and illicit passion was often lost, and once again, the news was bad for women. When Christian theologians slipped into dualistic thinking, women came out on the negative side of every duality: mind over body, spirit over flesh, reason over emotion, heaven over earth. The body, the fleshly nature, earthiness, and the emotions were inseparably linked with womanhood in the masculine mind, where Eve could be blamed for having caused the whole mess in the first place.

This was the legacy handed down by Christianity in its turn to the culture of the West, where it became dominant. The theological superstructure erected on these basic premises has been well documented by feminist theologians and historians, and does not need to be revisited here. But once women, the body, and the emotions had been linked and devalued, it remained only for post-Enlightenment thinkers to toss religion itself into the same bin.

From the earliest days of the social sciences, proponents of the "secularization hypothesis" have predicted that science, as a superior way of knowing, would increasingly displace religion, which would ultimately wither away. The early sociologist August Comte (1798–1857) predicted that religion would die out, and that clerics would be replaced as authority figures by scientists, especially by sociologists, since Comte considered sociology the "queen of the sciences." Sadly (speaking as a sociologist), his vision is yet to be fulfilled, but a more recent example comes from anthropologist Anthony Wallace, writing in 1966:

> The evolutionary future of religion is extinction. Belief in super-
> natural beings . . . will become only an interesting historical

memory. To be sure, this event is not likely to occur in the next generation; the process will very likely take several hundred years . . . But as a cultural trait, belief in supernatural powers is doomed to die out, all over the world, as a result of the increasing adequacy and diffusion of scientific knowledge.[9]

Although Wallace conveniently gave himself a few centuries before his prediction could be proved untrue, the continued high rates of belief and of religious participation in the United States and elsewhere suggest that if secularization theorists are going to predict the future, they're going to need some supernatural help.[10]

The Freudian school of psychology reduced religious belief to unconscious wish fulfillment, and a regression into infantile, magical thinking.[11] The dread of personal annihilation in death, together with an insurmountable sense of guilt, causes some people to retreat from reality and seek comfort in a God who constitutes an illusory parent figure. The idea that this powerful deity can be appealed to through religious rituals is a regression into superstition and magic.[12] In the Freudian system, women are particularly prone to erotically tinged wish fulfillment because their personality is "a harmonious blend of masochism, narcissism and passivity."[13] Thus religious experience, *particularly the more affective forms associated with female mysticism*, can be dismissively reduced to the neurotic wish fulfillment of hysterical women, as Sydney Callahan writes:

> Of course, in the eyes of unbelievers those males who report mystical experience also should be dismissed as deluded, but the common judgment was that one finds "affective and erotic forms of mysticism associated with women and more speculative or intellectual forms of mysticism associated with men." "Affective and erotic" elements are the problematic characteristics seen to infect women's religious experience.[14]

What it boils down to for Freud and those he's influenced, which includes most of the Western world, is that religious people are crazy, women are crazy, and religious women are especially crazy. Women, being weaker, are more prone than men to resort to religion as a flight from threatening reality, and the passionate expressions of religion that are most characteristic of women betray a frustrated sexual development. Here, as in the Greek philosophers, we see the cultural setup for a devaluation of the kataphatic, "affective and erotic" or passionate way of prayer, of which, as we'll see in chapter 4, women have been some of the foremost proponents. Yet as Callahan observes, there is a far more parsimonious explanation for women's tendency to experience the life of faith in such terms:

> Love of every kind, familial and erotic, must always have played a large part in female lives and socialization, so it is not surprising to find women using these images to express their love of God and God's love for creatures.[15]

The scientific value of parsimony calls for explanations to be as simple and straightforward as is consistent with the data. That women have long been socialized toward emotional expressiveness, and men away from it, is a simple, straightforward explanation for observed gender differences in spirituality, an explanation that does not resort to nebulous constructs like "masochism" and "magic." Of course there have been and are women whose prayer is more apophatic in nature, and men drawn to the kataphatic way. Further, the apophatic way has its own, more obscure, forms of passion, which we will explore in part 2.

Like all dichotomies, the "apophatic/kataphatic" opposition is oversimplified and potentially misleading, because every mature spiritual life will contain elements of both. At this point in my own development, which I would hardly call "mature," the two paths are both evident in my relationship to the different Persons of the Trinity. I tend to see the Father in an apophatic way, while I relate to the Son in a more kataphatic way; the

Spirit is within me, stoking the fire that propels me toward them both. The Father is "the King of the ages, immortal, invisible," "who has immortality and dwells in unapproachable light" (1 Tim 1:17; 6:16). I rarely pray directly to the Father, except when forced to by the liturgy, and then with a good bit of trembling. Jesus called his Father "Abba," and many people find comfort and reassurance in that familiarity, but mostly it's Jesus himself who is immediate and accessible to me—still awe-inspiring, but touchable, audible, knowable, the God who meets me in the hidden chambers of my soul. And in those depths the Spirit moves: prompting, teaching, closer than my pulse, tending the flame.

I can't vouch for the theology of all of this, but I am certain that in practice, the apophatic and kataphatic ways are not mutually exclusive, but complementary. An intimate relationship between humans will include both times of silence and times of speech. However deeply we love another person, and however powerfully that love may reduce us to silence, we cannot conduct an entire relationship in silence. And so we have moments of speechless awe, but we also sing, dance, make poetry, make jokes. Introverts will be more inclined to the silent admiration of their partner, and extraverts will be more talkative. But people who talk all the time are annoying, and people who never talk are weird. A normal intimate relationship includes both, and this is as true of relationships in the vertical dimension as those on the horizontal plane.

And yet, at an archetypal level, the apophatic and kataphatic paths do represent identifiably distinct spiritualities, even distinct vocations, one of which sees emotional exuberance as a distraction, while the other sees it as fulfillment. Developments in the larger culture have given these two paths a gendered dimension, and caused first one, then both, to be marginalized and devalued, as we have seen. But within the church, a parallel but distinct story has been unfolding, which also has implications for contemporary views of passionate mysticism. Let's examine this story briefly, and then we'll have a context for understanding the development of the tradition of spiritual passion itself.

A Passionate God and a Wary Church

Over the course of its history, the church has varied in its attitude toward mystical or contemplative prayer[16] in general, and toward affective or kataphatic prayer in particular. Ask three theologians what the term "contemplation" means and you'll get five different answers, which gives theology a lot in common with other branches of knowledge. In the spirit of St. Teresa of Avila's *Interior Castle*, I will define contemplation simply as prayer that is principally initiated and directed by God, rather than by the person praying. Prayer becomes contemplation when God takes over.[17] Definitions such as Thomas Keating's, which holds that contemplative prayer is "communing beyond words, thoughts, feelings, and the multiplication of particular acts,"[18] strike me as too restrictive. They rule out kataphatic prayer by definition, and rob God of half his repertoire. This is precisely the issue we're dealing with, of course, so let's not get ahead of ourselves. How did the church itself come to discourage contemplative prayer, especially in the kataphatic form?

From the early days of Christianity into the Middle Ages, prayer was understood to be the means by which all Christians, laypeople as well as clergy and religious, grew into an intimate, experiential knowledge of God. *Lectio divina*, or "divine reading," was a method developed to move a person from reading or hearing a passage of Scripture to discursive meditation[19] on the passage, to affective engagement with it, and finally to a quiet resting in the presence of God. All of these acts would be part of a single period of prayer, and all of them were available to all Christians.[20]

Among medieval mystics, affective prayer was highly valued, as were the supernatural phenomena (visions, "locutions" or voices, stigmata, and the like) that sometimes accompanied it.[21]

That these phenomena were taken as validating the mystic's claim to authenticity, and were consequently prized and sought after, meant that the church had to spend a good bit of energy distinguishing the genuine from the fake. Criteria for discernment were developed, but eventually sensible skepticism gave way to blanket discouragement and dismissal.[22] The Middle Ages had also seen the birth of the great schools of theology, and a new religious division of labor in which the "knowledge of God" pursued by theologians was heavily analytical in nature, while experiential knowledge was the realm of mystics. Both types of knowledge, as well as the deeper levels of prayer once open to all, were increasingly considered out of the reach of laypeople and, in time, even of most monks and nuns.[23]

By the sixteenth century, John of the Cross was encouraging people to simply disregard or forget any visions, locutions, or other events that occurred during prayer. Teresa of Avila, his friend and coconspirator in the Carmelite reform, tended to ignore this advice, though she did counsel caution and careful discernment under competent spiritual direction. Perhaps it was her gender that made Teresa more at home with extravagant expressions of emotion; in William James's manly judgment, "her idea of religion seems to have been that of an endless amatory flirtation . . . between the devotee and the deity."[24] Fortunately for Teresa, as the first woman Doctor of the Church her status is not particularly vulnerable to the judgment of William James. Of course, as the author of splendid poetry, John was no stranger to the emotions. But when it came to prayer, he shared the larger church's wariness of mystical "events."

Ignatius of Loyola, another great Spaniard of the same century, also tried to instruct the faithful in the deeper realms of prayer. Ignatius developed a method of prayer in his *Spiritual Exercises* that included discursive meditation, affective prayer, and the imaginative application of the senses to the subject of the meditation. Yet his own order quickly prohibited the practice of all but discursive meditation, trapping people close to the surface. Such was the influence of the Jesuits in the Roman

Catholic Church that Thomas Keating gives them a large share of the blame for the suppression of contemplative prayer in the church in the centuries that followed. It reached a point where even aspiring to contemplative prayer was considered presumptuous, and clergy and religious were actively discouraged from it, to say nothing of the laity.[25]

By the mid-twentieth century, the contemplative tradition in Christianity had been so well buried that spiritual seekers interested in meditation had to turn to the religions of the East, and any suggestion that they might learn about meditation or contemplation from the Christian tradition would have been met with genuine surprise. Thomas Keating, a Trappist monk, is at the center of a movement seeking to change that. He and other teachers of "centering prayer" have introduced many contemporary Christians to their own heritage of contemplative prayer, and we are just beginning to see how powerful prayer becomes when people enter the presence of God and *stop talking*. In fact, if I had only five words to teach people about prayer, I think "Show up and shut up" would do very nicely.[26]

The problem I see with centering prayer is that it leaves half the job undone. The two anti-mystical strands we have seen developing in the history of the church are its opposition to contemplation in general, and its opposition to kataphatic prayer in particular. Based in large part on the anonymous fourteenth-century mystical text *The Cloud of Unknowing*, centering prayer sits squarely in the apophatic tradition, in that it teaches people techniques for sitting in silent attentiveness to God, including how to deal with distracting thoughts and feelings. This is immensely helpful. The trouble, in my view, is that centering prayer defines *all* thoughts and feelings as distractions, including those that might actually come from God. Keating advises his students to reject them all:

> Let [your prayer] be a time of interior silence and nothing else. If God wants to speak to you in successive words, let Him do so during the other twenty three hours of the day.[27]

On a practical level, though, for most ordinary people living in the world there aren't twenty-three other hours to spend in complete attentiveness to God. Many of us are doing well if we can manage the one. To be fair, Keating emphasizes resting in silence because in the noisy contemporary world, this is probably the hardest thing to do, and the type of prayer that has been most neglected.[28] It is also true that masters of prayer are often more flexible than their students, and I've sometimes detected in Keating's disciples a rigidity less evident in his own work.

In practice, however, the centering prayer movement suffers from two problems:[29] First, the centering prayer method is taught to all comers, with no attempt to discern whether the individual's vocation is to the apophatic or the kataphatic path. Second, the kataphatic way is itself devalued, relegated to the earliest stages of spiritual development, a juvenile preoccupation with spiritual "toys" that will be put away with the other childish things when one reaches spiritual maturity, which is defined in narrowly apophatic terms.[30] As if misogynistic Greek philosophy, post-Enlightenment social science, and the Counter-Reformation weren't enough, the kataphatic mystic is covered with yet another layer of disapproval, and the pastoral consequences are serious, as Janet K. Ruffing makes clear:

> Too often, I have listened to the concerns of directees with many years of rich and varied religious experience wondering if or when they would ever reach the more highly valued apophatic experience of God. Too often, in supervising spiritual directors, I have felt their uncomfortableness with the voices, visions, feelings, and intensity of kataphatic directees and their desire to discourage these experiences rather than explore them.[31]

The result of this fearful rejection of the kataphatic way is that

> People whose path is primarily kataphatic continue to cut off their toes to try to make their feet fit the apophatic shoe. Some ignore the ways God is manifesting presence to them. Others

try to repress their rich imagery, flee their visions, or fear for their sanity. Some are reluctant to share their religious experience with spiritual directors for fear of being judged immature, self-centered, or unbalanced. They wonder if there is something wrong with them if after thirty or forty years of committed prayer and Christian life they do not seem to be resting in the imageless, conceptless *nada* advocated by apophatic teachers.[32]

Ruffing's research shows that in fact many mature adults who have a deep spiritual life, involving a serious and long-standing commitment to prayer, report that over the course of their lives kataphatic experiences deepened and expanded rather than giving way to "imageless, conceptless" silence.

Contrary to the assumptions of the more rigid teachers in the apophatic tradition, God has more than one trick up his sleeve. Our diversity is crucial to God's plan; in each of us he speaks a word about himself, and to force everyone into a rigid conformity is to drastically reduce the vocabulary of God. These teachers are correct when they say we should not seek spiritual consolations for their own sake; we should seek only God. But when God comes bearing spiritual gifts, we'd better be careful not to despise them. It's a desert God we seek, and we need to be ready to welcome him when he comes, whether he comes with hands full of flowers or of sand. Only if we're willing to meet him in either the desert or the oasis can we trust that our desire is holy. Passion manifests itself in both desire and darkness. We'll come to the darkness in due time, in this book as in life. For now, let's focus on how passion has been understood in the kataphatic tradition, especially in that form known as "love" or "nuptial mysticism," where the emphasis is on desire.

Desire of Ages, Ages of Desire

With the possible exception of Buddhism, virtually every religion has a tradition of love mysticism, in which mystics use the metaphor and language of romantic love to describe the soul's relationship to God.[33] Many writers of the Hebrew Scriptures understood the bond between God and Israel as a covenant between Bridegroom and bride: "your Maker is your husband, the LORD of hosts is his name" (Isa 54:5). God's sorrow over faithless Israel is depicted in terms of a cuckold husband: Israel has "played the whore" with other nations and their gods (Ezek 16; Hos 1–3). Indeed, she is worse than a prostitute, who at least is making a living; Israel is more like an adulterous wife, giving it away for free (Ezek 16:31-34). Yet as hurt and angry as God is, he is overcome with tenderness, and pledges not only to receive her back but to actively seek her, devising little schemes for drawing her back to him: "Therefore, I will now allure her, and bring her into the wilderness, and speak tenderly to her" (Hos 2:14). When he has won her back, and erased the names of her lovers from her memory, he promises: "I will take you for my wife forever" (Hos 2:19).

The ultimate example of love mysticism in the Hebrew Scriptures is, of course, the Song of Songs (or Song of Solomon).[34] "Let him kiss me with the kisses of his mouth," it begins, "for thy love is better than wine" (1:2 KJV). Because of its subject matter, both Jews and Christians have been uneasy over the inclusion of this book in the canon of sacred texts. The book is a set of poems consisting of exchanges between a pair of young lovers, with occasional antiphons provided by the "daughters of Jerusalem." Its imagery is intensely sensual and frankly erotic, and the entire book makes not one explicit mention of God. Yet the oldest Jewish reading of the Song casts God as the Bridegroom and Israel as the bride. Their longing is mutual; indeed, much of the action consists of the woman urgently seeking her lover. This is not some delicate little flower who bats her lashes behind her veil, but a grown woman with grown-up desire who asserts, "I am my beloved's and my beloved is mine"; "I am my beloved's, and his desire is for me" (6:3; 7:10).

It's more surprising that the Song made it into the canon at all than that there's been a long-standing ambivalence about it.

Ancient Jewish teachers maintained that the book should only be read after the age of thirty, and only then if the rest of the Scriptures had been read first. Yet Rabbi Akiva, the spiritual force behind the Jewish rebellion in 135 CE and a famous Torah scholar even today, taught that the Song of Songs was in fact the very heart of the canon, its Holy of Holies.[35] For Rabbi Akiva, the Song was a model for Israel, a challenge for them to approach God with that kind of passion, and he maintained that "the whole world realized its supreme purpose only on the day when the Song of Songs was given to Israel."[36]

The allegorical reading of the Song of Songs was picked up later by Christian writers; patristic authors such as Origen (d. ca. 253) identified God/Christ as the Bridegroom, and the bride as the church. Origen also acknowledged that the bride could represent the individual soul, an interpretation that would be brought to the fore by later mystical texts. Yet even patristic prissiness could not really get around the fact that the Song was first and on its face a piece of erotica:

> Awake, O north wind; and come, thou south; blow upon my garden, that the spices thereof may flow out. Let my beloved come into his garden, and eat his pleasant fruits. (4:16 KJV)

> My beloved extended his hand through the opening
>   and my feelings were aroused for him. (5:4 NASB)

With passages like these, it's no wonder that Origen, like the Jewish scholars before him, worried that the Song might be a bit much for immature readers. He emphasized the need for the bride to purify herself and her desire in order to be worthy of such a groom. Of course, Origen also castrated himself to avoid temptation, so we might consider his position on these matters a little extreme.[37] Yet for all his intellectualizing, Origen did celebrate the passion in the Song, and the passionate God it portrays: "I do not think one could be blamed if one called God Passionate Love (*eros/amor*)."[38]

The New Testament, too, has its share of nuptial imagery. The letter to the Ephesians famously assigns a deeper meaning to the bond between husband and wife, which the *Book of Common Prayer* picks up in the rite of holy matrimony, saying that marriage "signifies to us the mystery of the union between Christ and his church."[39] In his second letter to the Corinthians, Paul is worried that his converts in Corinth might be lured away by another: "I feel a divine jealousy for you, for I promised you in marriage to one husband, to present you as a chaste virgin to Christ" (11:2). The consummation is reached, as consummations typically were in those days, at the marriage supper of the Lamb in the book of Revelation, where the church is presented as a bride to Christ, the Bridegroom (chap. 19).

Love mysticism based on romantic bridal imagery reached its zenith in the Middle Ages. Bernard of Clairvaux (ca. 1090–1153), Cistercian abbot and one of the greatest scholarly minds of his time, delivered to his monks a series of sermons on the Song of Songs that greatly influenced Christian mystical theology and are still read today. Like earlier writers, Bernard thought the Song was best reserved for the spiritually mature, and only began his sermons after his monks had been instructed from the books of Ecclesiastes and Proverbs. Departing from earlier teachers, however, Bernard interpreted the Song as representing chiefly the relationship between Christ and the individual soul. He also dropped the earlier preoccupation with purification and virtue, and stressed the need of the soul to respond to God with passionate love:[40]

> O stormy, violent, burning, surging love who do not permit that one should think something other than you . . . You tear down orders, pay no heed to ancestry, know no measure. Propriety, reason, modesty, counsel, judgment—all these you make your prisoners.[41]

Mostly, Bernard emphasized the tenderness of God's love over its intensity, and commended this type of love to his monks.

The very idea of passion was already suspect, as we have seen, linked in the medieval mind with self-indulgence and uncontrolled worldly desires. And yet, try as he might to be circumspect, Bernard's own passion is impossible to miss:[42]

> I find no rest until he kisses me with the kiss of his mouth. I am grateful that I may kiss his feet, grateful also to kiss his hands. But if he likes me at all, he should kiss me with the kiss of his mouth. I am not ungrateful—but . . . I beg, I beseech, I implore: he should kiss me with the kiss of his mouth![43]

Bernard was not the only twelfth-century writer to emphasize the importance of love over intellect in the journey of the soul to God; others such as Hugh and Richard of St. Victor, and William of St. Thierry, also opposed the arch-intellectualism of the likes of Peter Abelard.[44] But Bernard's appropriation of the ideal of courtly love taking hold in European secular culture at that time, and his application of it to the soul's romance with God, proved a long stride forward in the development of mystical theology. It was immensely influential—most immediately, and most memorably, among a gifted group of thirteenth-century women known as the Beguines. I have already mentioned the Beguines in passing (see chapter 1), but they played such an important role in the development of love mysticism that we will want to consider that role in greater depth. In the next chapter, then, I invite you to get to know a remarkable group of women.

Chapter Four

The Beguines:
A Spooky Sisterhood

> While church and state no longer collude to burn heretics
> or hang witches, women's religious experiences can still
> be readily discounted. Not a lot has changed . . .
>
> —Sidney Callahan, *Women Who Hear Voices:*
> *The Challenge of Religious Experience*

Some of my closest girlfriends have been dead for eight hundred years. Fortunately, this does not really present a problem for our relationships. Granted, we can't go to the movies together, but then I don't really go to the movies much anyway. It's more fun to make up your own stories, which frees you to hike around the inner landscape where you don't have to listen to other people eating popcorn. For this sort of thing my family nicknamed me the "Spooky Kid," a name conferred with much affection but not a little bafflement. In our family, at least, it's not really the usual thing for little kids to climb up into the attic and spend the afternoon there by themselves. Extreme introverts were kind of thin on the ground at our house.

When I first encountered the Beguines, though, it was like finding footprints on that inner landscape, in territory I'd assumed to be unpopulated. In short, I stumbled upon a spooky sisterhood, a collection of women who understood, who *knew*, who'd lived long and well in that terrain and knew its contours intimately. Like many older women friends they were both companions and guides, mentoring me through experiences I could not have understood on my own. They were the best of company for the journey, because the Beguines were as intelligent, literate, passionate, and gutsy a group of women as you'd find anywhere, in any century. These women spoke the truth they knew, in beautiful and accessible language, without masculine or institutional protection, in a world where such behavior could cost you your life. The Beguines have been called the first Western women's movement;[1] they were called heretics and whores at the time. But they lived faithful to the gospel as they understood it, and their lives and works, long neglected, are beginning in our day to receive the attention they deserve.

A Movement of Holy Women

The twelfth and thirteenth centuries were a time of dramatic social change in Europe.[2] Advances in technology and trade created a massive growth of wealth and a surge of materialism. As the rise of the urban merchants and traders challenged the old feudal system, upward mobility and consumerism increasingly distanced their way of life from that of the growing mass of urban poor—a situation not unknown to us today. At the same time, a wave of religious fervor swept across Europe, bringing a new conviction that an adult participation in the life of faith was for all Christians: lay as well as clergy and religious, women as well as men.

The widening gap between elites and masses produced two reactions in medieval society: unrestrained consumption on the one hand, and renunciation on the other. Appalled by the lavish lifestyles of their neighbors, including those neighbors who were running the church, a growing body of clergy and laypeople embraced voluntary poverty and sought to return to the simplicity of the gospels. At the same time, the notion that the Christian life was the property of an elite of "professional Christians," while the role of the laity was limited to "pray, pay, and obey," was fast falling out of favor. More and more laypeople, including laywomen, felt drawn to the *vita apostolica*, the life of poverty and service to the poor modeled after the apostles.

Yet while a number of new religious orders had appeared in the twelfth century, by the thirteenth many of these were closing their doors to women. And while the mendicant orders (Dominican and Franciscan) that arose in the thirteenth century offered men the opportunity to pursue lives of poverty and service, they offered women mainly the cloister. Third orders arising out of the mendicant movements gave both men and women the option of living their charisms "in the world"; still the swelling ranks of women seeking to live by religious ideals presented the church with a demand it could not adequately supply.

It was in this context that the Beguines[3] appeared, mainly in Germany, France, and the Low Countries. The Beguines were an autonomous movement of laywomen[4] who took no vows and lived by no single Rule, but were dedicated to apostolic poverty, chastity, and acts of charity to the poor. These were not ladies' auxiliaries of existing men's orders, but a movement in their own right, though they had an affinity for the mendicant orders and often chose Franciscan or Dominican priests as their confessors. Beguines' status and living situations varied greatly. Early on, they were often single or widowed women living with their own or others' families, or married women whose husbands had agreed to a separation so that both might pursue the religious life. As time went on their houses increased in size and complexity, from a half dozen or so in a single dwelling to large communities ("beguinages") containing numerous individual houses as well as a church, brewery, hospital, cemetery—essentially, everything needed for independent little cities. As "semireligious," they represented a third way between the cloister and the world: between the restrictions of the convent and those of the house of father or husband, Beguines found a measure of freedom virtually unknown to women of their day.

They got away with it for about a hundred years. In the early years of the movement, the Beguines were widely admired for their holiness and their selfless service to the poor. In 1233, the famous preacher Jacques de Vitry obtained from Pope Gregory IX semiformal permission for the Beguines to continue living together for their mutual support and edification. Yet they had their enemies, including those who disliked the mendicant orders, those (and they were legion) who worried about heresy, and others who simply believed that women on their own would get up to no good. Their work, especially in the cloth industry, placed them in competition with the established guilds, which won them no friends among either the male members of those guilds or the women dependent on them.

By the middle of the thirteenth century, public opinion had turned against the Beguines. They were routinely confused with the Albigensians and other critics of the church and of the clergy. Most damaging of all, however, was the fact that gifted women among them were teaching, preaching, and writing on spiritual subjects in the vernacular, to lay audiences.[5] Given that women were widely believed to be intellectually and spiritually incapable of dealing with such subjects, this was too much for some clerics to bear, and opposition mounted. Despite their commitment to chastity, they were accused of sexual license and linked to the Brothers and Sisters of the Free Spirit, as well as other heresies. One of their most vociferous critics was William of Saint Amour, who argued that, being laywomen, they should be excommunicated for wearing habits and cutting their hair.

The heresy charges were to prove deadly. A Beguine named Aleydis was executed for heresy as early as 1236, which provoked an outcry from a public that still venerated the movement. By 1310, when Marguerite Porete was burned at the stake in Paris as a relapsed heretic for her work *The Mirror of Simple Souls*, the tide of public opinion had already turned against the Be-guines. The Council of Vienne (1311–12) concluded:

> We have been told that certain women commonly called Be-guines, afflicted by a kind of madness discuss the Holy Trinity and the divine essence, and express opinions on matters of faith and sacraments contrary to the catholic faith, deceiving many simple people. Since these women promise no obedience to anyone and do not renounce their property or profess an ap-proved Rule, they are certainly not "religious" although they wear a habit and are associated with such religious orders as they find congenial. . . . We have therefore decided and decreed with the approval of the Council that their way of life is to be permanently forbidden and altogether excluded from the Church of God.[6]

The council did include an escape clause, permitting faithful women to live chaste lives of penance and humility together, even without formal vows. But the combination of the council with the heresy trials of Marguerite Porete and Dominican Pro-vincial Meister Eckhart, who also wrote on spiritual matters in the vernacular, along with widespread suspicion and hostility among clerics and the public, took the steam out of the Beguine movement. By the fourteenth century, beguinages were increas-ingly populated by poor and uneducated women who did not occupy themselves with theological concerns. The movement never disappeared completely; according to Knuth, in 1969 there were eleven beguinages in Belgium and two in Holland,[7] and Murk-Jansen reported in 1998 that a young woman in Belgium had recently made vows as a Beguine.[8]

But the great legacy of the Beguine movement was generated in its heyday in the thirteenth century, when a gifted group of women created a remarkable body of writing that not only advanced mystical theology, but virtually created vernacular poetry and prose in several languages, and remains some of the most sublime work in those languages to this day. This spooky sisterhood built communities that ultimately proved vulnerable to the power of a threatened ecclesial hierarchy, but that sustained them for a time in the absence of institutional support. They wrote without male protectors, but also without male interference. They worked for a short while in a small space of freedom, but in that small, free space they gave voice to a passionate love for God. Eight hundred years later, they still have a lot to say to us, and contemporary writers are increasingly turning to these mystical texts to learn about the passion of the soul.

The Women

In the early days of the movement, Beguines tended to be drawn from the wealthier social strata in which fairly advanced learning was often provided to daughters as well as sons. In consequence, while not every Beguine was a poet or theologian, the overall intellectual level among them was quite high, and the standard of education offered at Beguine schools was elevated as well. Among the writers who did come out of the movement, four are especially noteworthy, and it is their works that will give us an introduction to the characteristic spirituality of the Beguines.[9]

Beatrijs of Nazareth (1200–1268) was a Cistercian nun who had been educated by Beguines and bore the stamp of that training for life. A pious little girl from a devout family, at age fifteen she took the Cistercian habit, and from age thirty-six until her death at sixty-eight, she was prioress of one of a collection of convents founded by her father after her mother's death. Beatrijs wrote one short work in Middle Dutch, *The Seven Manners of Love*, which chronicles the movement of Love (*Minne*) in her own life and represents the first treatment of mystic experience in the Brabant dialect. This account of her life is reinforced by a biography written by a priest who served as confessor at the Nazareth convent, and who identifies himself only as a "brother and companion in God's service."[10]

In contrast, no biography exists of Hadewijch of Antwerp, who most likely wrote in the first half of the thirteenth century and whose work is that of an extremely well educated, culti-vated, and skilled woman. She knew Latin and used courtly expressions extensively in her work, and her command of both theological and secular literature and learning was exceptional. On this basis, it seems safe to assume that she came from a noble or at least a very well-to-do family, though the details of that family and her likely place in it are a matter of considerable scholarly speculation. Her work is contained in five manuscripts that consist of forty-five poems in stanzas, a collection of other poems, thirty-one letters, fourteen visions, and a list of eighty-six "perfect ones"—people living or dead whom she most admired.

Hadewijch seems to have been the subject of some opposition during her lifetime, but among our four Beguines only Marguerite Porete paid for her writing with her life. An out-spoken critic of the established church with a reckless tendency to blow off its hierarchy, Marguerite inevitably attracted the attention of the Inquisition, which uncovered evidence of heresy in her book *The Mirror of Simple Souls.* The book was burned and readers were threatened with excommunication; Marguerite was declared a heretic, imprisoned in Paris for eighteen months, ordered to recant before an ecclesiastical court, and threatened with death. When she refused to appear, she was declared a relapsed heretic by the Inquisition and handed over to the secular authorities. She was burned at the stake in what is now the Place de l'Hôtel de Ville in Paris, and impressed the gath-ered crowd with her courage. In the end, it was probably not so much heresy that led to her death as her audacity in writing in the vernacular. As Saskia Murk-Jansen has observed, within a hundred years Marguerite's work was being widely circulated all over Europe, attributed to an unknown Carthusian monk: "Ascribed to an anonymous male member of an Order known for its severity and conservatism the book was acceptable, even admired; written by a lay woman it was deeply suspect." [11]

Mechthild of Magdeburg (ca. 1207–1294) died in her bed about fifteen years before Marguerite's execution, but she knew the risks she took with her own book, *The Flowing Light of the Godhead*:

> I was warned against writing this book.
> People said:
> If one did not watch out,
> It could be burned.[12]

When Mechthild confronts God with the danger, pointing out that "you are the one who told me to write it," God responds:

> My dear One, do not be overly troubled.
> No one can burn the truth.[13]

One can't help noticing that God makes no promises about whether the *bearers* of truth can be burned. Fortunately for Mechthild's readers, she seems to have been satisfied with the reassurance she got, and went ahead with the project despite the danger.

Mechthild also came from an affluent family and was well educated, though not as well as Hadewijch, which does nothing to detract from her charm:

> Now my German fails me; I do not know Latin. If there is something of merit here, it is not my doing; for there never was a dog so nasty that it would not come if its master coaxed it with a white breakfast roll.[14]

Mechthild entered the Beguine community at Magdeburg in her mid-twenties. For many years she concealed her mystical experiences, but finally told them to her confessor, who encouraged her to write them down. Mechthild's book is actually a collection of seven books of poetry and prose in multiple genres; she is, among our Beguines, the foremost exponent of "bridal" or "nuptial" mysticism.

As the movement began to lose support among both clergy and the public, Mechthild followed the path of many other

Beguines, and took refuge in the arms of an established religious order. In her sixties, she moved into the Cistercian convent at Helfta, which was quite a little mystic farm in its own right. As death approached, she knew both the infirmity of old age and the desolation of spiritual darkness. But she was surrounded by women who respected her, and she at least had the satisfaction of living to see a book by William of Saint Amour, archenemy of the Beguine movement, ordered burned by the pope.[15]

The Works

The genius of the Beguines was to adapt the literature of courtly love to the relationship between the soul and God. They were not alone in finding their spiritual models in the mythology of courtly romance; the myth itself had religious components, in the purity of the knight and of his quest, the incorporation of sacred elements such as the holy grail, and so on.[16] Other mystics of the time also drew upon this tradition, notably Francis of Assisi, troubadour in the service of Lady Poverty. But the Beguines raised these themes to new literary and theological heights in the school of *minne-mystiek* (love mysticism), and they also engaged in some creative gender-bending reminiscent of Bernard of Clairvaux.

For Bernard, nuptial imagery, in which his own soul took the role of bride, involved an "imaginative inversion"[17] from male to female, as well as from active to passive and from higher status to low. For a Beguine such as Mechthild it is status alone that's inverted, because she remained in the feminine role but in the courtly myth the noble woman a knight serves is his superior. For Mechthild, as for Bernard, Christ as the male lover is clearly superior. Other Beguines, such as Hadewijch, inverted gender instead of status, seeing themselves as humble, powerless knights in the service of divine Love (*Minne*, which is feminine in both Dutch and German):[18]

> Love has subjugated me:
> To me this is no surprise,
> For she is strong, and I am weak.
> She makes me
> Unfree of myself,
> Continually against my will.
> She does with me what she wishes;
> Nothing of myself remains to me;
>   Formerly I was rich,
> Now I am poor: everything is lost in love.[19]

The soul willing to embark on the chivalrous adventure will be tested to the utmost: in the service of passion, it will certainly not be bored. As Beatrijs put it:

> Love leaves her neither peace, not respite, nor rest. Love raises her up and casts her down, suddenly draws her close only to torment her later, makes her die to bring her back to life again, wounds her and heals her, drives her to madness and then makes her wise again. It is in this way that Love draws her to a higher state.[20]

Service to the lady Minne takes courage; the soul will have to risk everything, and endure many trials along the way. In part 3, I will explore the suffering borne in the service of Love in greater depth. But while Love is a demanding and exacting mistress, she knows how to reward her admirers. To Hadewijch, Minne promises:

> "I will cherish you;
> I am what I was in times past;
> Now fall into my arms,
> And taste my rich teaching!"[21]

Within the overarching category of love mysticism, which is the hallmark of Beguine spirituality, specifically nuptial imagery traces out a special theology of desire. In bridal mysticism, the soul longs for God, and the satisfaction of this longing is sometimes described in pretty vivid terms. In one of Hadewijch's visions, Jesus first gives himself to her "in the shape of the Sacrament." Afterward,

> he came himself to me, took me entirely in his arms, and pressed me to him; and all my members felt his in full felicity, in accordance with the desire of my heart and my humanity. So I was outwardly satisfied and fully transported.[22]

The soul longs for God, but Mechthild in particular stresses that God also longs passionately for the human soul. He tells her:

> Your secret sighs shall reach me.
> Your heart's anguish can compel me.
> Your sweet pursuit shall so exhaust me
> That I shall yearn to cool myself
> In your limpid soul,
> To which I have been bound . . .
> I cannot be without you.
> No matter how far we are apart,
> We can still never be really separated.[23]

There is a deep and perhaps surprising mutuality here between the soul and God where, as Hadewijch says, "Beloved and loved one shall wholly flow through each other."[24] Christ himself instructed Mechthild on this point, telling her:

> I longed for you before the beginning of the world. I long for you and you long for me. Where two burning desires meet, there love is perfect.[25]

For the Beguines, the purpose of a person's life is to become increasingly accustomed to being immersed in love. The soul is like a crab trap in the water, and the water is God. The trap and the water are two different things, but in union they come to occupy the same space, and the water flows freely through the trap, filling it entirely with itself. Many mystics have also spoken of an "exchange of hearts" in which Christ seals his union with the beloved soul;[26] this too is the language of mutuality. Janet Ruffing has identified mutuality between God and the beloved soul as a sign of transforming union, "the goal of the spiritual journey short of resurrection."[27] It is the supreme intimacy that the soul and God both long for (and that we will explore in chapter 9), and Mechthild's description of this intimacy is unsurpassed in the literature of nuptial mysticism:

> Then the bride of all delights goes to the Fairest of lovers in the secret chamber of the invisible Godhead. There she finds the bed and the abode of love prepared by God in a manner beyond what is human. Our Lord speaks:
>
> "Stay, Lady Soul."
> "What do you bid me, Lord?"
> "Take off your clothes."
> "Lord, what will happen to me then?"
> "Lady Soul, you are so utterly formed to my nature
> That not the slightest thing can be between you and me.
> Never was an angel so glorious
> That to him was granted for one hour
> What is given to you for eternity.
> And so you must cast off from you
> Both fear and shame and all external virtues.
> Rather, those alone that you carry within yourself
> Shall you foster forever.
> These are your noble longing
> And your boundless desire.
> These I shall fulfill forever
> With my limitless lavishness."
> "Lord, now I am a naked soul
> And you in yourself are a well-adorned God.
> Our shared lot is eternal life
> Without death."
> Then a blessed stillness
> That both desire comes over them.
> He surrenders himself to her,
> And she surrenders herself to him.[28]

This is the sort of language one often finds in mystical texts that can leave the reader not knowing where to look. But let's be clear on what Mechthild is talking about here. Jesus does not literally want her to take off her clothes; after all, being God, he could presumably see through them if he wanted to. Mechthild is reaching for language that will describe her experience, and as so many other mystics have found, the language that comes closest and serves best is that of erotic love. Jesus doesn't literally want her naked, but Mechthild uses this imagery because there is nothing that describes the soul's nakedness before God quite like—well, nakedness. Someone once remarked to me that there are very few English teachers among fundamentalists, because literary people understand metaphor and analogy. I don't know if that's true, but then, perhaps he didn't mean to be taken literally. The point is that mystics who describe their experience in romantic or erotic terms are not intending these images to be taken literally; they're not talking about genitalia here. They're talking about an intimacy of spirit that is ineffable. There is no language that can adequately describe what they nevertheless feel compelled to communicate.

And so, like the more apophatically oriented language of paradox, which uses terms like "unknowing," "unfaith," and "radiant darkness" to express the inexpressible, for kataphatic mystics erotic language points in the direction of loving mystery, mysterious love. To understand mystic texts correctly, we need to get beyond our clunky literalism, raise our attention above our navels, and see that we are being invited to something not less than, but greater than, human love. It's not that Mechthild and the others are not going that far; they are going further, speaking of desires and satisfactions that human love knows only at a distance, only as something fleeting, caught out of the corner of the eye and then gone. Religion, as my social science colleagues remind us, has existed in all societies and at all times because humans have needs that cannot be satisfied with the resources of this world.[29] Religious people will nod in comprehension; we are built that way for a reason, so that our unsatisfied desire will drive us relentlessly toward God. An ancient Norwegian legend has it that when God creates a human soul, he plants a kiss on it that remains with it forever.[30] There's a lot of truth in that story. Myths are stories that are truer than they first appear, and the mystics who speak of God romancing the soul are presenting us with "big truth," a truth too large to be mastered; it can only be served.

The kiss of God on the human soul leaves, according to the legend, a deep memory of the One who bestowed it. When God connects with a person at any level, whether through creation, through baptism or transforming union, what's done there cannot be undone; the bond remains forever. The tie can be broken, though not without violence; such ruptures tend to leave ragged edges. But once made, the connection cannot be unmade as if it had never existed. The bell, as they say, cannot be unrung. This is why, although as even C. S. Lewis noted, most mystics will resort to erotic language sooner or later, another form desire takes is nostalgia: in Lewis's words, "our longing to be reunited with something in the universe from which we now feel cut off, to be on the inside of some door which we have always seen from the outside, [which] is no mere neurotic fancy, but the truest index of our real situation."[31]

The Welsh have a very useful word, *hiraeth*, which refers to "the sense of loss that comes with having been separated from one's home; missing the feeling of being home, of having a place."[32] This word *hiraeth* is pregnant with theology; to borrow Lewis's phrase, it is the truest index of our real situation. We were made for God, to dwell with and in God. When we come face-to-face with Christ, we come home; more than just where we were meant to live, this is where we come from, this is our *source*. God is our true home, our origin and our destination, our going out and our coming in, as the psalmist says.[33] But we have been broken, separated and sent into exile. So our lives are a story of God's unceasing labor to bring us home, to his own embrace where we began, in that moment of the kiss upon the soul. Elsewhere I have written of discovering that heaven is not a place, but a Person.[34] God is the place we come from, and our hearts will be suffused with desire—well disguised at times, to be sure—until we return there.

This longing for a home we can scarcely remember, our baffling patriotism for a country we've never seen, was well known to our ancient spiritual forebears. In the letter to the Hebrews, the author writes of Abraham, Sarah, and other heroes of the faith:

> All of these died in faith without having received the promises, but from a distance they saw and greeted them. They confessed that they were strangers and foreigners on the earth, for *people who speak this way make it clear that they are seeking a homeland.* If they had been thinking of the land that they had left behind, they would have had opportunity to return. But as it is, they desire a better country, that is, a heavenly one. (Heb 11:13-16; emphasis added)

"From a distance they saw"—and we see too, through a stirring piece of music, perhaps, or a dramatic sunset, or the innocence in the face of a child; we see something that reminds us of home. These fleeting reminders, these "shafts of glory,"[35] arouse us to hope but also contain a poignant reminder of the anguish of separation. Separation is the essence of hell, which is why grief is the emotion closest to despair: the permanence of separation through death is a pain almost beyond human endurance. But separation from home is also a great grief, and our Beguines understood this. Beatrijs wrote of the bitterness of the soul's longing for God:

> That is why her life on the earth is henceforth a complete exile, a narrow prison and excruciating suffering . . . it brings her great torments to be a stranger in a distant land. She cannot forget her exile and she cannot satisfy her desire, while her nostalgia distresses her. Hers is a merciless passion and torment, beyond all measure.[36]

The problem of exile, of separation, is, after all, the central problem addressed by religion. The word "religion" actually comes from the Latin for "re-bind" or "re-tie"—to establish again a connection that's been broken. For the Beguines, the spiritual journey consisted of the return of the soul to its original dignity, its original being in God.[37] As Hadewijch put it:

> And so it is that He has raised us up and drawn us by His divine power and His human justice towards our original dignity, rendering us the freedom in which we were first created and loved by God, thus confirming His call and establishing our election in which he had foreseen us from all eternity.[38]

Mechthild shares this vision of the soul's destiny as a return to intimacy with God, which she expresses with her characteristic charm. When the character Contemplation suggests that Mechthild's humanity places her in a less exalted position than that of the angels, Mechthild retorts:

> When the game is over, then let one see how the scales tip . . . Jesus Christ, who soars above the Seraphim, who is undivided with his Father, Him shall I, the least of souls, take in my arms, eat him and drink him, and have my way with him. This can never happen to the angels. No matter how high he dwells above me, his Godhead shall never be so distant that I cannot constantly entwine my limbs with him; and so I shall never cool off. What, then, do I care what the angels experience?[39]

Marguerite Porete portrays the soul's return to God as "annihilation." The soul dissolves into God, and loses its own identity, as when a river empties out into the sea:[40]

> SOUL: Ah, most sweet, pure, and divine Love, what a suave transformation it is to be transformed into what I love more than myself. And I am so transformed that I have lost my name in order to love, I who can love so little; it is into Love that I have been transformed; for I love nothing but Love.[41]

Marguerite is right: the return of the soul to God requires a radical transformation, and in that transformation we increasingly partake in God's very nature, which is love. At journey's end, "we will be like him" (1 John 3:2), and share in his glory (1 Pet 5:1). If we aren't shocked by these assertions, we aren't taking them seriously. But this has been God's plan all along. When the Beguines speak of God raising us up to our original dignity, what they're saying is that the ugly-duckling-turned-swan story is another "big truth." If there really are only seven stories behind all of literature, this is undoubtedly one of them, the story of transformation, the discovery of great beauty under a layer of obscuring filth. "Cinderella" is a classic version of this. We could update it a bit and call it "The Princess Turned Crack Whore Who Marries the King." I can just see him, stooping down to pull his thoroughly trashed bride out of the gutter, and shooing away the clientele. He takes her home, subjects her to the full-scale spa treatment (purgation), and before she's gotten over the shock or even achieved full sobriety, the vows have been exchanged.

It's a great story; in fact, it's *the* great story, another version of the good news (which, incidentally, is also told in the book of the prophet Hosea). Hadewijch's line that God is "establishing our election *in which he had foreseen us from all eternity*" reminds me that God was never fooled by the dirt. However deep and however ugly, he could always see past it, to the person he made us to be, knew us to be, at the moment of that first kiss. The problem for many of us is that we have neither the vision nor the imagination to see past our own dirt. But this is, again, because we don't take the gospels seriously. Return to the transfiguration, where Jesus revealed to his closest friends, and through them to us, who he really is: God from God, as we say in the Creed, Light from Light. And the disciples who saw that uncreated light on Mount Tabor were dazzled into incoherence.

But what else did Jesus teach us about light? "The eye is the lamp of the body"—the connection to the light. "So, if your eye is healthy, your whole body will be full of light" (Matt 6:22). If our connection to the light is strong, then we ourselves will be filled with light, radiant, shining like the sun. What Hadewijch and the other Beguines are saying is that God can see that radiance through the smudges and rags, and perhaps, if we will just look at Jesus long enough and steadily enough, we will see a new image of ourselves, this sparkle of light, reflected in his eyes. And that next kiss, when it comes, will leave us with a mouth full of stars.

Desire of the kind the Beguines wrote about can be overpowering, overwhelming, at times frightening, and even a bit embarrassing. One thing that may not be immediately obvious, though, is that intense desire is also purifying. A person whose whole being is consumed with longing for one thing is not thinking of anything but the object of that desire: home, the beloved, or whatever it may be. As Søren Kierkegaard said, "Purity of heart is to will *one* thing." When we will one thing so completely that that desire eclipses all others, even for a moment, we become pure in heart. And it is only the pure in heart who really see God; that is how Minne rewards those who suffer for her. To see God is to die, of course. But dying to our old, limited selves and being resurrected to a new and unimagined level of existence is, after all, what the life of faith is all about. It's what we signed up for in baptism, and the surprise for us is that God takes it, and us, far more seriously than we'd dared to hope.

My spooky sisters have taught me a lot. They've shown me a little of what it means to love passionately and live dangerously. They've shown me where, or rather Who, my true home is, and made me understand why exile can be so excruciating at times. And they've convinced me that God is in the transformation business, and if he sometimes does his remodeling with a wrecking ball, at least when he's done, he's not going to "flip" me:

he intends to live here himself, forever. I understand this a little better for having been in the company of such extraordinary mentors: "bold women," as one admirer wrote, "who remind us why we were born." [42]

Chapter Five

Postmodern Passion:
The Many Vocabularies
of Desire

> Only connect! That was the whole of her sermon. Only connect the prose and the passion, and both will be exalted.
>
> —E. M. Forster, *Howards End*

The Beguine movement produced some wise and gifted writers, and as we have seen, they had a lot to teach us on the subject of desire. But let's face it: they're getting kind of old. How do people experience and speak of desire in our time? What are the longings of our day, and with what vocabularies—if any—do we describe our journey into God?

A *USA Today/*Gallup poll conducted in 2002 showed that about a third of adult Americans describe themselves as "spiritual but not religious."[1] People who do see themselves as "religious" don't tend to have a lot of time for this position. In a book whose title and author I've long forgotten, a priest commented that "'Spiritual' does not make hospice calls." A little spin around the internet turned up similar comments:[2]

- Spiritual but not religious means you're too lazy to read a book but still want to act like a flake.

- Being spiritual instead of religious means that you get to sleep in on Sunday morning.

- I always took spiritual but not religious as meaning a moral person without serious beliefs who will have sex on the second date.

- Is this like smoking pot but not inhaling?

It's easy, and very tempting, for religious people to dismiss the "spirituality" of the spiritual but not religious. We seem to suspect that the description indicates a desire to experience good feelings, and lay smug claim to a higher consciousness, without any of the pesky discipline and accountability that goes with religious commitment. All bliss and no bloody sweat, as it were. Knowing God, we may even be a little worried that these slackers will get their paycheck at the end of the shift, just like those of us who have borne the heat of the day.[3]

Perhaps a bit of posturing and commitment phobia do lie somewhere behind the "spiritual but not religious" identification for many. Without access to their inner motivations, I can only say that what most people seem to mean by this phrase is that they feel drawn to a deeper existence, beyond the demands of the body, the ego, and conventional society, but they don't feel drawn to "organized religion." People who are moved by music, or paintings, or who feel most alive in the mountains, know that there's more to life than work and toys. They just don't see a connection between the stirrings of their soul in those moments and the act of sitting through a religious service. And it's not just that institutional religion is irrelevant; it's more than that. If these people haven't actually been burned themselves by the church, they've heard, as we all have, horrendous stories of how it has wounded innocents within and without, through history and in our own time. If people don't feel that their hunger can be fed at our table, can we blame them?

And yet, they do hunger. For what? Christians often want to tell people what they desire, to put it into traditional religious language that contains the correct categories, which will point folks toward the conventional religious answers. But that wasn't Jesus' way. In John's gospel (1:38), the first thing Jesus says to the first people who come to him is, "What are you looking for?" He's just been baptized, and a voice from heaven has identified him as the Son of God. John the Baptist has declared him "the Lamb of God who takes away the sin of the world" (John 1:29, 36). People are looking at him expectantly, hardly daring to hope. You'd think that when a couple of John's disciples run up behind Jesus after that and call him "Teacher," Jesus would start *teaching* them, would tell them what they need to know. But instead of leading with his own agenda, Jesus asks them, "What are you looking for?"[4]

They didn't give him a straight answer. They didn't say, "Well duh, we're looking for the messiah, and we were sort of hoping it might be you." Considering that this man might well be the next king of Israel, this was probably a prudent choice. Instead, they kind of shuffled around (one imagines), and finally managed to bleat out, "Well, ah . . . Rabbi . . . where do you live?" If they didn't give a straight answer, I suspect it's because they couldn't. Of course, like all of Israel they were looking for the messiah, but that's really just a shorthand way of saying that they had all kinds of hopes and dreams that they could barely articulate, and they hoped to find someone who could fulfill them.

How like us that sounds. The human condition doesn't change much, but some things do change, and one of them is the vocabulary our culture gives us for expressing our hopes and dreams. In first-century Palestine, if you felt restless and dissatisfied and longed for something more, most likely you'd speak of foreign occupation and the hope for the promised messiah. In medieval Europe, where the myth of courtly love was one of the dominant "stories" of the culture, a man could express his sense of restlessness and longing as a desire to distinguish himself in heroic service to a noble lady. Not so helpful for the medieval woman, perhaps, yet as we have seen, some devout women, as well as men, made creative use of that same vocabulary by turning it to the intimate bond between the soul and God.

Different times and cultures provide different languages to speak of restless longing and a desire to live at a deeper level. In our time, many writers are rediscovering the language of love mysticism, and we will consider their work shortly. But for many people in our day this traditional language is unintelligible. As Ronald Rolheiser has observed, somewhere along the way our culture seems to have made a pact in which religion and eros were separated.[5] We live, says Rolheiser,

> in a broken situation. Religion, especially as it is lived out in the churches, is perceived as being antierotic, antisex, anticreative, antienjoyment, and anti-this-world. The God who underwrites the churches is then perceived as stoic, celibate, dull, cold, otherworldly, and threatened by sex and by human creativity. The secular world is seen as the champion of eros, sex, creativity, and enjoyment, but is seen as anti-God and antichurch.[6]

God certainly seems to have come out the loser in this transaction: passion goes to the secular world, and God gets left with a cold, thin gruel called "religion." It's said that every generation thinks it invented passion; it's equally true that every generation forgets that God invented it. We look at God the way we look at our parents, naïvely imagining that they know nothing of what's going on in our hearts. And like confused adolescents, we can scarcely say ourselves what is going on there.

I would argue, however, that our deepest restlessness and dissatisfaction stems from a desire for *connection*, which exists in two dimensions: the horizontal and the vertical. Again, there's a lot of variation across time and cultures in how people express these desires, and considerable variation too in how intensely people experience them. As with other appetites, some people are voracious, while others get by on very little. In any case, let's look at each of these dimensions in turn, and consider some of the vocabularies of desire available in our culture that are not explicitly derived from traditional Western religion. Then, having recognized and examined some of the other ways of feeling and expressing desire, we will be ready to look specifically at expressions of religious desire, especially those that make use of the language and imagery of love mysticism.

Secular Vocabularies of Desire: Reaching Out, Reaching Up

We know that we are social creatures; we know it theologically, sociologically, biologically. Even those of us who are born hermits, and prefer our own company to most anyone else's, find that just that little bit of solitude beyond what we actually want can fill us with loneliness and dread. And what do we do when we manage to get time to ourselves? Log into Facebook, read an online forum, turn on the TV, plug into our iPods—anything to connect to another human being.

Throughout our history as a species, we have needed each other to survive. So the desire to connect in the horizontal plane goes deep within us, and perhaps the most primal version of horizontal desire is sex. Indeed, French courtesans of the nineteenth century were called *les grandes horizontales*, skillfully managing the horizontal connection both figuratively and literally. Of course, sexual desire has always been with us, but what has changed is the limits on sexual behavior in our post-sexual revolution society. Once reliable birth control divorced recreation from procreation, we were free to wear tie-dyed T-shirts and ratty jeans, and do what people dressed like that do. And so we went on doing it, imagining ourselves "liberated," until

AIDS came along and reminded us that we are still not really in control.[7]

The sexual revolution changed some things, but we are still faced with the basic human dilemma of simultaneously wanting and fearing to be known. Now that we have more sexual options, there are new and interesting ways to lie to ourselves about this predicament. Casual sex means you can have a feeling of closeness, but you can always go home before he finds out that you snore. James Taylor wrote a song called "Is That the Way You Look?" The lyrics are a little cryptic, but my husband likes to think it's the lament of a guy who's awakened next to his latest, and is seeing her for the first time without the paint and props. It may be even more frightening for her than for him. Real intimacy requires getting past that moment, and the many moments of self-disclosure that will follow. But casual sex is cheap intimacy. It's like doing it in the dark with all your clothes on: it bears a certain relationship to lovemaking, but it's kind of neurotic and cumbersome. Alternatively, it's emotional cotton candy, and there's only so much you can eat before the regret sets in.

Apart from sex, one of the most powerful languages of horizontal connection in our society is the language of "community." Elsewhere[8] I have written of how deeply the idea of community resonates with contemporary urban and suburban folk. We look back wistfully at small town life of the past, where neighbors knew and looked after one another, where there was always a welcome and a cup of coffee next door. In these fits of nostalgia, we're apt to forget the realities of small town life: the kids on meth, the eyes behind the curtain, the impossibility of change—individual or corporate.

In a rather different mood, people with elaborate tattoos, piercings, and other forms of body modification sometimes speak of building a new community, or "tribe," with its own culture in which conventional ideas of beauty are rejected. As a twenty-something blogger writes:

> My Body Modifications have opened countless doors to endless self expression, and for almost a decade, flesh and fashion have been my own personal playground. But for me, the beauty of Body Modification is more than superficial, there's a rebelliousness in it because it comes at the expense of public ideals of beauty. People who are getting pierced are following their personal aesthetics, and not popular ones.[9]

The snag is, of course, that tattoos and piercings are enormously popular, and are not much more original than the uniform my friends and I wore at that age. But notice that rebelliousness and individualism are not this young man's only goal:

> I quickly found myself dedicated to the cultivation, preservation, and integration of community, through an emerging Body Modification culture. In an era based upon independence, intolerance, and division, the human heart is awakening to a modern vision of community through a new depth of interpersonal relationship.[10]

The writer's second goal is to cultivate an alternative community with its own culture— that is, he wants to belong to something, wants precisely *not* to be unique. Sociologist Mary Waters[11] has commented on how the most successful advertising campaigns send the consumer two messages at once. On the one hand, if you buy this product, you will distinguish yourself as a unique and discerning individual. On the other hand, we assure you that your unique and discerning taste is validated by countless others who have made the same choice, so get on board!

I haven't made a study of it, but my guess is that in those shrinking parts of the world where most people still do live in small communities, the word "community" probably isn't used that much. The idea of community is most appealing to those of us in alienated, postindustrial societies, where the reality of community is so distant that its symbolic power is correspondingly increased. In anonymous urban America, we're so enamored of community that we use the word promiscuously, speaking of "the gymnastics community," "the horse-racing community," "the 2003 silver Volkswagen Jetta community."

Community is important, particularly for racial, sexual, and other minority groups, whose survival in a hostile society depends on solidarity. But the rest of us often fail to notice how intrusive that solidarity can be. My husband, like me, is an academic. Unlike me, however, he is African American, and one thing I've seen over the years is how much extra work he does because of this. Every committee on campus wants people of color "represented," and because there are so few of them, they all do more committee work than the rest of us. Every hour they spend on committee work is an hour they aren't doing the research that will advance their careers. Further, graduate students of color want to see someone who looks like them on their committees, which means more time spent away from research. Finally, the larger ethnic community expects that these scholars will "give something back," and they often have very specific expectations about the form that giving should take. The more successful one is, the less likely it is that these expectations will ever be satisfied.

As a white academic, I face none of these demands, and if I choose to "give back," I have the prerogative to decide for myself where and how much I will give. Mary Waters[12] points out that whites often look to their ethnicity for a sense of community, which is harmless enough unless we start equating our ethnic experience with that of people of color. Anyone who thinks that being Irish American is like being African American or Mexican American or Korean American is missing the fact that for whites, ethnicity satisfies the twin demands of the perfect ad campaign. It offers one a chance to be interestingly different (Irish—indeed, almost anything—is more interesting than "white"), while at the same time being part of a group with a common heritage. Most important, this misses the fact that for whites, ethnic community is costless; it's belonging to a club that requires no dues. Perhaps ethnicity for whites is a bit like casual sex: you can feel close to others without having to give too much away.

I don't mean to disparage ethnic identity for white people; there are certain things about my own identity that I quite enjoy. (Being mostly German and English, obviously traditional cuisine is not one of them.) But it is a little bit like being "spiritual but not religious." There is a definite need within us to connect to other people, and if we can get that connection at a low price, many of us will take it. But it turns out that you do get what you pay for, and cheap intimacy, whether in the bedroom or the Sons of Norway Hall, ends up being pretty superficial. For some people, it's enough. But for those whose appetite for horizontal connection is more demanding, a more demanding connection is going to be needed.

Human beings also need to connect in the vertical dimension, though for many of us this need is less obvious than our need to connect socially. Religion is all about connections, of course; recall that the word "religion" means to link again, to reconnect. I can't speak for religions of the East, but in Western monotheism, at least, connections to God and to fellow humans are seen as mutually reinforcing. Still, the vertical dimension takes primacy: in the words of the Westminster Catechism, "Man's chief end is to glorify God and to enjoy him forever." But I am suggesting that even those who are not religious, or even spiritual, have desires that reach upward as well as outward. How might these desires be experienced and expressed?

I've said that ethnicity, for whites and people of color, can be a means of reaching out to others. But for people of color particularly, I think it can also be a way of reaching up. I teach university courses on race and ethnic relations, and over the years I've watched these young people come to college and experience a shift of consciousness as their identity becomes politicized. Often these kids' experience of "celebrating diversity" so far has consisted of tacos in the school cafeteria on

Cinco de Mayo, and black history contained within a single month (because everyone knows that black people only ever did anything important in February). At college, though, they are given the analytical tools for a more rigorous examination of ethnic and racial history and politics in America, plus some solidarity with co-ethnic students and faculty, and the effect can be electrifying.

For such students, identity politics can become a functional alternative to religion. That is, it serves many of the same purposes as religion: it tells them where they come from and who they are; it gives them a community, to be sure, but it also makes them part of something larger than themselves. It gives them a sense of meaning and purpose, something to live for, to sacrifice for, and in certain times and for certain people, something to suffer and die for.

Other social and political movements and moments can also give people a sense that they're participating in something significant. One of the reasons for Barack Obama's success in the 2008 presidential election is that he relentlessly took the high road. Whether his presidency will keep to that road remains to be seen, and there are plenty of good people who, for whatever reason, didn't support him. But when Obama spoke to voters, he spoke to their highest values, and asked them to be true to those values. He called to our nobler nature, and the response to that call among people of different races, classes, regions, and political persuasions showed that tribe can be transcended when we reach for something higher.

We can also reach for something lower, namely, the ground under our feet. Many people's passion expresses itself in a concern for the earth; for some, religion plays no part in this concern, while others find within various religious traditions vocabularies for describing our ties to and responsibility for the planet we inhabit. The Judeo-Christian tradition tells us that God created the earth and gave humans the job of looking after it. Francis of Assisi's affection for the earth is one of the reasons people like me are still attracted to him eight centuries after his death. Unfortunately, however, for most of its history Christendom's idea of looking after the earth has been to grab what we can out of it and not think about the consequences.

Given this sorry record, it's no wonder the church speaks with little credibility when it comes to caring for the planet. Native American spirituality is a more attractive alternative to many, who sense in it a wisdom and closeness to the earth with none of the baggage of Christianity. This path is not without its problems, however. First, the origins of this image of Native peoples lie partly in reality, but also in stereotypes of Indians as "noble savages," which simultaneously romanticize their connection to the earth and dismiss them as relics of the past, with no relevance or role in the modern world.

Second, "Native American" is a category invented by Europeans, and imposed on hundreds of separate peoples. So it's fair to say that there is no one "Native American" spirituality, yet many non-Natives, unaware of distinctions between nations or tribes, borrow from various traditions in ways that don't make much sense. Imagine a Chinese person who's attracted to Western spirituality: she has a menorah in the window, a crucifix on the door, and wears a hijab while celebrating the Eucharist all alone, with chips and a Diet Coke. I've been told again and again that this is a bit what it looks like to Indians when others dabble in their traditions. Take a peace pipe, add a bit of drumming, and finish in a sweat lodge, and voilà, you're deeply spiritual. While genuine interest in Native religion is often given a warm welcome, superficial culture-poaching and mindless syncretism are deeply resented by many Native people, and it's not hard to understand why.

Whether we approach other traditions as seekers or as shoppers, Americans' interest in religious alternatives does suggest that many of us are looking for spiritual connections that seem unavailable in our own traditions. Of course, many of us aren't looking for anything of the kind. Yet one thing that virtually all humans seek, whether they're religious, spiritual, or neither, is meaning. Yes, there are a few existential nihilists around, but when was the last time you met one? If we don't seek meaning in God, we may seek it in our children, or in service to humanity, and we have a vocabulary for this too: we speak of "making a difference." And we honor those who've made a difference; whether we call them saints or heroes or role models, we look up to them and what they stand for. And in looking up, we connect to them—vertically.

We seek meaning in the negatives too: a natural disaster or a grim diagnosis will invariably be met with the question, Why? We wonder why innocent people get drowned by tsunamis, or why vegetarians have heart attacks. There's an implicit sense of justice violated; as a species, we are not easily reconciled to randomness. Along with our awareness of our own mortality, the need to make meaning is what separates us from the rest of the animal kingdom, and of course, the thing we ultimately need to see the meaning of is our mortality. Most of us put that off as long as we can, but in the meantime we are constantly trying to make sense of the events of our lives and our times.

Sacred Vocabularies of Desire

The point I'm trying to make by talking about connecting in the horizontal and vertical dimensions is that whether we are spiritual, religious, both, or neither, we all experience in some form and to some degree the desire for connections. We need to feel tied to other people, and to something beyond the surface routines of our lives, and we need ways to speak of that desire. Secular culture provides us with language and imagery to express those needs. Certain symbols, such as "community" and "making a difference," resonate deeply with many, if not most of us, while others such as "ethnicity" or a given political movement will be less widely shared.

In the same way, religious traditions provide language and imagery that help us communicate those experiences that are among the hardest to articulate. Christian culture, like secular culture, has a rich store of metaphors to convey those things that are most important, yet correspondingly difficult to express. Further, as is the case with secular culture, religious metaphors will resonate more with some people than with others. The image of God as "father" is a good example of this. Jesus spoke often of his "father," and Christians through the ages have followed that example. Yet for those people whose earthly fathers were emotionally harsh or physically abusive, the idea of God as "father" doesn't work so well. Likewise, Jesus spoke of himself as the "good shepherd," but what does that mean to people who've never seen a sheep that wasn't wrapped in plastic and sold by the pound?

There are other Christian symbols that are less problematic, and that we go to again and again: life as a pilgrimage, the mountaintop experience, the desert wilderness, the dark night of the soul. We have our images for the highs and lows of the spiritual life, and most of us have our favorites, though we make use of them all from time to time. These images have their different moods: the high of the mountaintop, the aridity of the desert, the lostness and confusion of the night, all stops on the pilgrimage whose destination is the heart of God. This is the language of intimacy, of (as St. Bonaventure put it) the soul's journey into God.

The farther we travel on that journey, and the nearer we get to our divine destination, the more inadequate our language and imagery become. This is where the path tends to diverge into two directions, as we have seen: for the apophatic soul, the language of intimacy speaks of darkness, silence, unknowing. This path takes us through a severe landscape, and we will examine this terrain more closely in chapter 8. For those on the kataphatic path, the landscape is lush and fertile, full of showy flowers and ripe fruits. While apophatic mystics know that Jesus did a lot of his praying in the wilderness, kataphatic mystics remember that God's original idea was to place humans in a garden and live intimately with them there.

This distinction, like the distinction between vertical and horizontal connections, is actually pretty artificial. As I said earlier, every pilgrim's path will take him or her through both types of terrain in time. But each of these spiritual "styles" has its own preferred language. As apophatic souls draw closer to God, and find language becoming increasingly inadequate, they tend to speak the language of paradox: radiant darkness, unfaith, God as *nada*, as no-thing. Not surprisingly, as kataphatic souls attain greater intimacy with God, they have an abundance of images with which to describe it. Yet most of them eventually make use of the language of romantic love. We have already seen how some medieval writers employed that language to express their experience of the numinous. For the remainder of this chapter, let's examine how contemporary writers have continued this tradition.

Reclaiming the Language of Love

It's easy to dismiss love mysticism as one of the many weirdnesses of the Middle Ages. And God knows, there were many: hair shirts, self-flagellation, the fetishizing of virginity, capital punishment for sex with the woman on top. Perhaps this notion of a love affair with God speaks more of a lifetime of sexual repression than of devotion, of celibate religious who had a lot of sexual energy to deal with and limited options for expressing it.

Maybe that was part of the story. I mean, when Catherine of Siena claimed that Jesus espoused her to himself and gave her his foreskin as a ring, you have to wonder. As one of the "holy anorexics," Catherine was a little weird in any case, and yet this strange, illiterate medieval woman spoke hard truths to popes and princes, and got them to behave when no one else could. Catherine was not a nun, not cloistered; she was a Third Order Dominican (or "Tertiary"), and as such lived "in the world," although she made a personal vow of celibacy at an early age.

Bernard of Clairvaux and the Beguines whose work we examined earlier were all, as far as we know, lifelong celibates.

But that was not true of all the medievals who contributed to the tradition of love mysticism. The Franciscan Tertiary Angela of Foligno (ca. 1248–1309), that "swooning, bedded saint,"[13] had known married love, and likely unmarried love as well.[14] And yet, like Catherine of Siena, Angela experienced the spiritual marriage to Christ. On pilgrimage in Assisi, she was looking at a stained-glass window in which St. Francis was being embraced by Jesus. "I heard him telling me: 'Thus I will hold you closely to me and much more closely than can be observed with the eyes of the body. And now the time has come, sweet daughter, my temple, my delight, to fulfill my promise to you.'" After the brief trip back to Foligno, Christ continued: "You are holding the ring of my love. From now on you are engaged to me and you will never leave me."[15] The ring, in this case, seems to have been made of conventional materials.

So Angela was not a lifelong celibate, though she does seem to have been a reasonably chaste widow by the time she experienced mystical union with Christ. And to be honest, Angela was pretty weird too: for example, she seems to have dealt with her overheated parts by applying literal fire to them. I mean, it was a strange time. But what about now? I've said that there are a number of authors in our time who are reclaiming the tradition of nuptial mysticism, and many of these have informed my own thinking on the subject. Some of them are celibate clergy or religious; these include Ronald Rolheiser, OMI (*The Holy Longing: The Search for a Christian Spirituality*), and Janet K. Ruffing, RSM (*Spiritual Direction: Beyond the Beginnings*). Most, however, have mates, or children, or both: Sandra Lommasson ("Tending the Sacred Fire: Sexuality and Spiritual Direction"), Elizabeth A. Dreyer (*Passionate Spirituality: Hildegard of Bingen and Hadewijch of Brabant*), Tara Soughers (*Falling In Love with God: Passion, Prayer, and the Song of Songs*), Wendy Farley (*The Wounding and Healing of Desire: Weaving*

Heaven and Earth), and John Michael Talbot (*The Lover and Beloved: A Way of Franciscan Prayer*). These writers cannot be dismissed as frustrated celibates looking to Jesus as the divine Boyfriend.

Why make use of romantic imagery? What is it good for? It might be useful to ask, first, what is any imagery good for? Why is it useful to compare things to other things? A simple example might help us here. When I was writing my doctoral dissertation, my husband, who is both an academic and a runner, often spoke of dissertations as marathons. Yes, they both take a long time. But beyond that, there are certain insights to be gained from the comparison. Because a marathon takes so long, you should be sure you really want to complete it; it's not something to be done on a whim. Because running 26.2 miles places such demands on the body, it's not enough to run long; you have to run smart. You have to understand some things about the changes the body will go through at different stages of the race. You have to pace yourself; this is not a sprint. And one of his favorite sayings about marathons is that when you reach mile twenty, you're halfway there. Likewise, a dissertation is a demanding, long-term project that takes planning and preparation, that will put the writer through certain changes, and it takes at least as much energy to sustain oneself through the final stage as it took to get there. Just as many people who start marathons don't finish them, many bright graduate students never manage to finish their dissertations. You have to run strong *and* smart, and you might as well accept that some of the things that will determine whether you finish are beyond your control.

So what do we learn by comparing the soul's relationship to God to the relationship between lovers? Yes, the focus is on the love. But if we sit attentively with this comparison for a while, we can learn some things that might well surprise us. As in a love affair, the initial rush of intense feelings is typically followed by a letdown, when things cool off and there's a temptation to move on. (More on this in chapter 8.) But if lovers stay together past this point, they will discover a deeper intimacy that is far richer than the excitement that accompanies novelty. Still, the passion in a relationship should be transformed, should mature; it shouldn't turn cold, it shouldn't die. If it does, the relationship is in trouble, and this is as true in the spiritual realm as elsewhere.

What else do we know about how lovers behave? For one thing, lovers don't think about each other for an hour a week; they think of each other constantly. When you're in love, you don't make plans without considering what the other might have planned, or what his or her preferences might be. If the person you love does something wrong, you're not going to take satisfaction in it, or go into a rage. If you really love this person, you're going to be sad, you're going to hurt for the person, to share his or her regret, and you're going to want to set things right and move on as soon as possible. Love, after all, "does not rejoice in wrongdoing,"[16] but it shoulders the burden of sadness as if it were our own.

If someone is rude to your partner, you take that personally too, and typically respond with indignation. If your partner is rude, however, you tend to give him or her the benefit of the doubt. If some guy cuts me off in traffic, I'm likely to think him an inconsiderate jerk. But if that guy turns out to be my husband, I'll probably be thinking, "Ah, poor guy, he's had a really long day"—unless I've had a really long day too, in which case I might think he's a jerk, but I'll probably get over it. Being human, we don't always love in the ideal ways, but when we're leading with love (rather than ego or other motivations), this is how we behave. A lot of people could benefit from meditating on what each of these observations tells us about a close relationship with God—the God they imagine is waiting for them to screw up, so he can send them to hell.

There's plenty more: for some reason, the more serious love relationships become, the more we want to make them public.

We know we sound ridiculous when we talk about how we feel, but somehow we can't help ourselves; the vocabulary of love is not very dignified. This is as true of heavenly love as of the earthly kind, which I suppose is where the concept of "holy fools" comes from. In any case, when we're in love, we not only want to make it public; we want to make it permanent. A "friend with privileges" may satisfy up to a point, but once love invades the relationship, most of us are going to want to pledge undying faithfulness. We want to grow old together; at least, if we have to grow old, we'd rather do it with each other than without. We want to please each other, want to give gifts to each other, and want to get as close to each other as the boundaries of the human body will allow.

One of the remarkable things about intimacy is that as our relationships become more significant, the things we share become more trivial. A man in a serious relationship doesn't just know his partner's politics, or that she likes opera and hates jazz. He knows where she buys her groceries, what kind of toothpaste she uses, what she eats for breakfast. When I can't remember some insignificant little thing about my husband, like his shirt size or which of his eyes is partially blind, we joke about how we're going to get through the immigration interview where they try to figure out whether it's a real marriage or someone is in it for the green card. Not knowing that I'm afflicted with terminal cluelessness, the ICE[17] agents will undoubtedly send me back where I came from. Since that happens to be southern Spain, I'd be okay with that. But only if my man can come too.

One of the most startling and moving insights I've gained from this imagery is that, in a romantic relationship, the desire is strong on *both* sides. Perhaps that sounds obvious, but for those of us who struggle with a diminished sense of self, this is so very hard to believe. As I've said, I believed for years that God loved me, but only because, since God *is* love, he really couldn't do otherwise. God was limited by his own nature, otherwise he would have shown some sense and some taste, and despised me as much as I did. It was only after spending a long time with the romantic metaphor that it occurred to me that when people are in love, they see the object of their love as beautiful. They know the other is human and has faults—at least in theory. But those faults seem a very small part of the overall picture. I used to go into confession weeping and gnashing my teeth, but that has changed. The last time, I confessed that I was still guilty of the same old stuff, "but somehow I just don't think God is all that fussed about it." The priest agreed; it's good to have a confessor who's more of a spiritual grown-up than I am.

As we learned from the Beguines, the gift of contemplation is a transformed identity. God is like any lover, and sees the object of his love as beautiful. He's not stupid, and he's not limited; he knows we're broken. But when we look into the eyes of Jesus long enough, and steadily enough, the image we will see reflected in that gaze is his picture of us, not our own. And his picture will take our breath away; as Janet Ruffing has said, "All that we do in spiritual practice—either through scriptural contemplation of the mysteries of faith and the reality of Jesus or through centering prayer [i.e., whether kataphatic or apophatic practice]—*leads to the experience of God's desiring us.*" [18] Ruffing goes on to show that this transformation of identity, this sense of ourselves as desired by God, is a necessary step toward a sublime mutuality between the soul and God:

> When intimate self-disclosure is mutual, both partners reveal themselves and receive the other without fusion or flight. For such intimacy to develop, however, feelings of inequality, either related to power or desire for one another, must eventually be overcome. Because God is by nature transcendent, we first experience God as dramatically, numinously, and powerfully Other. Few of us quite grasp that the process of mystical transformation gradually overcomes this sense of the utter Otherness of God in favor of a radical mutuality with God. [19]

Again, human relationships teach us that intimacy is hampered when one partner chronically thinks of himself or herself as unworthy. Of course, we are all unworthy before God. But there's a time to focus on that, and a time to let it recede into the background, and focus on God. As in any relationship, it's going to work best if each party brings a whole self to it. This is why we continually wish each other "Peace"—"Shalom," "Salaam," that state of wholeness, of complete well-being: God wants to restore us to that wholeness so we can look him in the face:

> When our two souls stand up erect and strong,
> Face to face, silent, drawing nigh and nigher,
> Until the lengthening wings break into fire . . .[20]

Elizabeth Barrett Browning's sonnet is a picture of human love that beautifully conveys also the mutuality of mystical union, a subject we'll return to in chapter 9. This is an image of what God wants for us, what God wants *with* us, the process of replacing our stony heart with a heart of flesh.[21] This is true whether our prayer is apophatic or kataphatic. Whether we find God in the cloud of unknowing or on the dance floor with a rose between our teeth, God calls us to draw closer until our wings break into fire. This fire of passionate longing, though painful and at times undignified, is the key to our salvation from a life of quiet desperation, of "superficiality, mediocrity, and what Walter Brueggemann calls 'under-living.'"[22]

You can sometimes get a good sense of what people mean by a concept by looking at what they define as its opposite. We considered earlier whether the mystics who wrote of passionate desire were just sexually repressed celibates. But the opposite of passion isn't celibacy; the opposite of passion is apathy, indifference, sadness, a loss of interest, of purpose, and ultimately, of the self. The term for this is "acedia," which we tend to translate as "sloth," but acedia is far more than simple laziness.[23] C. S. Lewis captured it brilliantly in *The Screwtape Letters*: when we move restlessly from one activity to another, seeking distraction, or when we idle our engines, doing nothing in particular but getting no rest from it, we have slipped into a perilous state indeed. There's a reason why acedia is one of the seven deadly sins, though perhaps it would be more accurate to call it a "deadly temptation."

A "sin of the long haul,"[24] the desert monastics called acedia the "noonday demon," because it hits you in the middle of the day, or the middle of your life, when you've been at it (whatever "it" is) for a while but the end is nowhere in sight. Academic terms reliably have the same rhythm: there's a point around midterm when the energy level in the classroom plummets, and both students and teacher are losing the will to live. Acedia invites us to give up, to move on, to slide into enervating escapism, or a lack of focus that dissipates our resources by sending them out into all directions. If, halfway through the quarter, I'm thinking of how much better life would be in the corporate world, or how I should have gone to law school, or fantasizing about winning the lottery, I'm hardly giving my best to my students, who will waste no time in matching my indifference with their own. Likewise, if I'm draining my spiritual energies thinking of how amazing I'd be as a pastor, or in urban ministry, or tending AIDS orphans in Africa, or if I'm just sitting in my pew thinking about lunch, I'm not giving my best to God, but sliding into a mediocrity of the soul.

Passion is the answer to this. Passion keeps our focus on the "one thing [that] is necessary,"[25] willing the one thing with an intensity that purifies our heart. It is in that purified, focused state that we can enter into intimate mutuality, and "see God" face-to-face, our souls erect and strong. This is the ultimate connection, the purpose for which we were created, the fulfillment of the two great commandments, in which vertical and horizontal converge into one love. It's the pearl of great price, the treasure hidden in the field. If we believe what Jesus told us, we'll sell everything to buy it, however reckless and foolish we look.

So how do we do that? How do we light a fire that looks like it's gone out, or maybe was never lit to begin with? The first thing to remember is that passion is not primarily a set of feelings. All of us enter into dark, arid places (a theme we'll examine in detail in chapter 8), and if we've learned anything from Mother Teresa, it's that some of the holiest among us spend the most time there. Warm fuzzies are not the measure of spiritual stature; the surest measure we know is how consistently we recognize Christ in the least and lowest, and treat them accordingly.[26] There are times when a sense of God's absence and abandonment are part of the process of growing up spiritually, and it's important not to fight against that process.

But that doesn't mean that we can't express to God our desire for closeness, and for a sense of his presence. The important thing, however, is not to *feel* close, but to *be* close. I think there are three things to keep in mind if we feel our passion is a little feeble. First, if we ask God to increase our love for him, and to draw us closer, I am convinced that this prayer will never be denied. It's asking for a fish, and God is not going to give us a stone, although some fish do look remarkably like stones. Second, if we want to see ourselves transformed in the eyes of Christ, we need to spend time looking at him; there is no shortcut around prayer. Finally, whatever does or doesn't happen, I've always found that "fake it till you make it" is a good rule. I don't mean pretending to be something you're not, but that if you're praying to be closer to God, do the things you would do if you were closer to God, to the extent that you can. The parable of the talents tells us that if we're faithful with what we've been given, however little it might be, we will enter into God's joy,[27] where all our longings are satisfied, and every desire fulfilled.

In the meantime, though, don't be too quick to despise the pain. All of the proponents of love mysticism attest to the fact that a passion for God brings suffering and desire together to a point where they become inseparable. In Hadewijch's words:

As Love's arrows strike it
    It shudders that it lives.
At all times when the arrow strikes
It increases the wound and brings torment.
All who love know well
    That these must ever be one:
Sweetness or pain, or both together,
    Tempestuous before the countenance of Love
. . .
Longing keeps the wound open and undressed
Because Love stormily inflames them.[28]

God's desire to satisfy our longing is infinitely greater than our longing itself. The hitch about this desire, of course, is that "the more sweetly it is quenched, the more insatiably it thirsts."[29] The soul that falls for God is in for a wild ride. And the wilder it gets, the more inadequate our vocabularies become. There comes a point where there are no words, and when that time comes, the "Spirit intercedes with sighs too deep for words,"[30] and we fall into silent surrender. Elizabeth Barrett Browning's sonnet speaks of a "deep, dear silence,"[31] where even the songs of angels just get in the way. When the songs fade out, and the ground falls away beneath our feet, then there remains only the velvety silence, a stillness echoing with the presence of God. When that time comes, there is nothing left to do but become fire.

Part II

Suffering

Chapter Six

The Problem of Evil
and the Problem of Ease

De profundis clamavi ad te, Domine.
Out of the depths have I cried unto thee, O Lord.

—Psalm 130:1

This morning, news broadcasts were reporting on a house fire in Pittsburgh that killed five children, from two to seven years old.[1] Along with two eight-year-old survivors, the five who died had allegedly been left in the care of a teenaged baby-sitter, who has either disappeared or never existed. A neighbor reported hearing the children's cries from within the house: "They were screaming, and five minutes later they stopped screaming." The two boys who escaped stood on the street begging for someone to help, but the flames had already made impassable the stairs to the second floor where their brothers and sisters were trapped.

There is so much suffering in this single story. To begin with, the physical agony of the children as they died such a terrible death. The chaos and confusion as the house came down around them, the one place they could expect to be safe. The helplessness and horror of the children and neighbor on the street and, one assumes, the remorse, shame, and fear of the sitter, if she exists.[2] How will the parents make sense of a loss like this, on such a scale? In the midst of their shock and grief, they will likely be consumed with anger: at the surviving boys for apparently starting the fire by playing with matches; at the sitter for her negligence or, worse, at themselves for leaving the kids alone; at God for letting it all happen.

I'm a teacher, and as I look over the content of my undergraduate courses, it strikes me that the one theme that runs through them all is suffering. In my introductory sociology course, I teach three units: one examines equality of access to education; one looks at global inequalities and asks how big are the gaps between rich and poor countries, how do we explain them, and what are the human consequences; and the third examines severely divided societies and the prospects for conflict resolution and peace building in countries torn by violence. My course on race and ethnicity focuses, predictably, on issues of inequality, prejudice, and discrimination.

Finally, I teach a course officially called "Comparative Social Problems," but unofficially we call it "Gloom and Doom." It includes three types of problems, and we study at least two cases of each: epidemics (the Black Death in fourteenth-century Europe and the AIDS crisis in Africa); genocide (multiple cases, but especially the genocides in Rwanda and Darfur); and slavery (in the ancient world, in the Americas, and contemporary slavery around the world). We learn, for instance, that there are countries in Africa where the life expectancy has dropped below age forty because of AIDS. We see video footage of Hutus hacking Tutsis to death with a machete. And we read a few of the stories of the estimated twenty-seven million slaves in the world today, like the girl from a small African village who moved to Paris with the family of a diplomat. They promised her an education, but instead she was held captive in their apartment, given her meals from the trash can, forbidden to go outside, and allowed only a few hours of sleep a night. When she displeased her "masters," she was beaten with electrical cord, and they crushed hot peppers and inserted them into her vagina.[3]

I tell people that I try to get the students through ten weeks of "Gloom and Doom" without resorting to antidepressants, and I do keep close tabs on how they're dealing with the emotionally draining material. But in fact, it is my objective in this course, as in the others, to force students to come face-to-face with the suffering of the world. This pedagogical priority sort of snuck up on me. I'm not sure when I decided that no one would get out of my classes without a stiff shot of reality, but I've been teaching that way for several years now. Some of my students come from suffering parts of the world, and they seem to appreciate having these stories told. But most of them are young and reasonably carefree Americans, who would not normally spend a lot of time thinking about these things. Jesus said that he would take personally what we did to and for the least of his people, and I guess I've decided that while others may be called to help them more directly, my job is to make sure that they are not invisible and forgotten. My students will not be allowed to ignore them, anyway—at least for the ten weeks they're stuck with me.

But what do we do with this information? How do we cope with the evil we see, even from a distance, even for such a short time? Many people, including many Christians, struggle mightily to accept the classic Christian answer to what philosophers call the problem of evil: how does a God who is good, loving, and omnipotent allow suffering to exist in the world he has made? Why does he not prevent it, or at the very least, punish it in ways we could see and understand? The classic answer is that God created us with free will, and does not force us to do good or stop us from doing evil because he seeks a relationship with us that is consensual, not coercive. Because we have been given the supreme dignity of choice, and because we choose evil, at least part of the time, we are broken people and our brokenness pervades all of creation. In Christ, God has entered into that brokenness and will heal the break in the fullness of time; this is what is meant by redemption, and this is the "good news."

I've always been able to accept that answer, but then I haven't lost five children in a tragic accident, or been beaten with electrical cord. I expect if I had, nothing would make sense to me, least of all abstract bits of theology that seem designed to let God off the hook when he could have prevented the loss of innocent lives. As I write this, I'm awaiting word on whether the lump on my dog's leg is benign or malignant, and it's amazing to me how quickly I can lose sight of my fine theology, and go spiritually primal. I've had several biopsies myself, and have had some bad medical news in my time. But none of these forced me to my knees like the thought of losing my dog. My *dog*, for God's sake, not my husband or sister, not my mom or dad. I begged God to let her be okay, and as I did I thought of all the children who have prayed that prayer for a parent, and the parents who have prayed it for a child. And I know that the world is full of people who prayed for all they were worth, and God was silent.[4]

Suffering enters every human life that lasts long enough. But most of us will not know suffering on a level the parents of the dead children in Pittsburgh will experience in the days and years to come—to say nothing of the places in the world where virtually the whole population is deeply traumatized by genocide, civil war, famine, disaster, and disease. There is an instinctive reverence in the face of such suffering that makes talking about it almost indecent if you haven't been there. I haven't seen my neighbors hacked to death by Hutus with machetes, slaughtered by the Nazis, swept away by tsunamis, orphaned by AIDS, or blown up by the IRA or the UFF, so what right do I have to talk about suffering? Do I even have a right to my own suffering, here in my peaceful, affluent corner of the world?

Not long ago, I was discussing the subject of suffering with a friend who's done a lot of it lately. Recently widowed and troubled with poor health, he's had ample occasion to meditate on the subject. I confessed that while I could understand the meaning of suffering for the faith, or for voluntarily depriving oneself to accommodate or even save another, I was having a hard time with the types of suffering that didn't have some obvious benefit; in what sense could such suffering be "redemptive," as I'd heard it called? I admitted that I was struggling to make sense of it, and my friend said, "That's because you haven't suffered." This surprised me coming from him, because he knows all about the darker periods earlier in my life, about my flirtations with despair.

And yet, though I expected a different take from him, I've tended to share my friend's view that I "haven't suffered." Being a middle-class white American isn't exactly a recipe for suffering; being female doesn't count because it's not as bad as being black, or Haitian, or a quadriplegic, or whatever (though I can't see that argument being popular among rape victims). Certainly there are all kinds of suffering in the world, but only those that are physical, or those that are caused by poverty or racism, can be taken seriously. That pretty much rules out anything I've experienced or am likely to in the foreseeable future. So while God might take pity on AIDS orphans and victims of genocide, he can't possibly take seriously any pain I might feel. God's compassion is for other people. Maybe God himself is for other people.

Sometimes you have to push an idea as far as it'll go to see how stupid it is. Doing that, I'm startled by my own simple-mindedness, as well as my lousy memory: I'd forgotten what someone who experienced "real" suffering had to say on this very subject, which I'd read years ago. In his book *Man's Search for Meaning*, Holocaust survivor and psychiatrist Viktor Frankl tells of a woman who consulted him, but was reluctant to discuss her problems in view of what Frankl had suffered in the loss of his family and his own imprisonment at Auschwitz and elsewhere. But Frankl didn't use his suffering to "trump" hers;

instead, he drew an image from his Holocaust experience to show her the validity of her own pain. He explained that suffering is like a gas: pumped into a chamber large or small, it will fill the space completely and evenly. As a more recent writer put it, suffering

> has no scale. In the midst of the most terrible national and international suffering, our own personal sufferings persist, and they are no less significant for not making the nightly news . . . No one—least of all God—requires that our pain reach a certain magnitude before it is worth noticing. The minimum number of persons who must be affected by a catastrophe in order for it to count is one.[5]

So the objective magnitude of the injury is not the point; suffering is entirely relative, and will get our attention whether it's a broken leg or a broken life. Viktor Frankl's response to his patient is astonishing for both its compassion and its wisdom. We can and should put our pain in perspective by remembering the suffering of others, especially those who are most defenseless and vulnerable. But Frankl, as a Holocaust survivor, had the moral authority to give us "permission" to feel our pain, as pain, and not as something less significant. In this I believe his voice is prophetic, that he speaks to us for God.

So we have God's permission to take our own suffering seriously, but are we prepared to let God off the hook for allowing human suffering to occur? Let's return to the problem of evil, and see if we really accept that an all-powerful, good, and loving God can permit the existence of suffering in the world. There are those who don't believe that God acts in human affairs, or indeed that God exists at all. Let's leave them aside for the moment, and assume that the gospel is true, that God's love for the world is great enough to act in a way that cost him deeply. If God was willing to take human flesh and then allow himself to be tortured, humiliated, and executed for our sakes, if he cared enough about our situation to pay the ultimate price to correct it, then why did he not step in and stop Hitler, Stalin, Pol Pot? If he chooses not to cure my cardiac arrhythmia, I can live with that—or so my doctor assures me. But why did he not save the five innocent children in that Pittsburgh house fire?

We expect a God who is just and merciful to act differently; what would it look like if he did? Perhaps we'd like him to strike the architects of genocide dead before they could carry out their plans. What would I have done about Hitler, if I were God? My first thought is to have a bus run him down in the street before he could become chancellor of Germany, but then that would have traumatized the bus driver, not to mention the passengers and onlookers. So a nice brain tumor, perhaps, or a roaring case of TB or tertiary syphilis would have done the trick. These fantasies can be quite entertaining if you enter into the spirit of them. I spent much of my adolescence in a country where unwelcome attention from strange men was a fact of everyday life for foreign girls. My friends and I used to enjoy the thought of an angel with a flaming sword relieving these guys of their genitals as we passed by—a *very* satisfying fantasy, that. And the Bible only encouraged us: think of King Herod, who persecuted the early church. On an occasion when his ego got completely out of control (Acts 12), God struck him dead and he was eaten by worms on the spot. And the people cried out, "Bravo, God! Encore!" But God, it seems, is very sparing with his encores. This is true as a general rule, and is especially true when it comes to striking the wicked dead before they can do more harm.

Why is that? This question has tied legions of theologians in knots over the centuries, and I am not going to untie it or them here. But I suspect that part of the answer has to do with the question, who are the wicked? This is where Christians look down and start shifting from one foot to the other, because we've been told we can judge acts but not people. People's equations, that is, the set of factors that lie behind their decisions and behaviors, contain too many unknowns to be solved by us mortals. If I lose my temper and hit my child, anyone can judge that action as wrong. But what factors led up to that action? Perhaps spanking in anger is the only model of discipline I ever learned. And perhaps the toilet's overflowing, all my bills are overdue, I'm on day two of a furious migraine, I'm a single parent of three, and at the moment this kid is being an unholy little brat. Does my equation, and my culpability, look different now?

I don't know. We can't even solve our own equations, much less anyone else's. God could presumably have grabbed hold of the raised arm of the Hutu preparing to take a machete to his Tutsi neighbor. But that moment came about in part because Hutu resentment built during years of Tutsi oppression and violence; at what step along the way do we expect God to act? We'd like to see God stop cold a gang member who's about to kill an innocent bystander, but what about all the people who brutalized him on the path to this act? What if those people are us?—unthinking, maybe even unwilling, beneficiaries of a system that makes life easier for affluent whites and continually degrades and humiliates poor people of color? Can I solve his equation? And what about sins of omission? I'd be happy to see God strike down the slaveholders who keep children in bondage, but I'm not so ready to be struck down myself when I'm too ignorant to distinguish between products made with slave labor and free, too busy to inform myself about global slavery, or too selfish to support the organizations that work against it.

We don't know what our own equations look like to God. All we can know is that all have fallen, including ourselves. My parish priest began his Good Friday sermon one year by asking, "Who was responsible for the death of Christ?" I came very close to raising my hand and shouting, "Me! I did it!" Being an academic, however, I recognize a rhetorical question when I see one, and stayed in my seat while he considered the roles played by the Romans, the Jewish authorities, Judas, and the crowds. Still, though my theological training doesn't go very deep, I do at least get that we all participated in the crucifixion, which is why Christian anti-Semitism has never made any sense to me. Besides the fact that it's tantamount to calling your grandmother a slut, the whole point of the Passion narrative is that we *all* did it. So to call Jews "Christ killers" is simply to call them brethren and fellow humans.

Hitler manifestly did not get that. Maybe his theological training was even sketchier than mine. The point, however, is that an all-powerful, just, and loving God could have stopped Hitler before he committed his evil, but wouldn't that same divine nature cause him to stop me before I commit mine? Where does a completely holy God draw the line between evil that should be stopped and evil that shouldn't? And again, what would that look like, what would be the result if God not only prevented Hitler from doing the harm within his reach, but also prevented me from doing the harm within mine? Suppose I'm having an argument with my husband. We have always been very gentle with each other's vulnerable spots, but some people will go straight for the jugular, and no one can hit that target with the deadly accuracy of a spouse. So what if I'm about to run my sword straight through the unprotected spot, where it will cause real damage? Should God strike me dead before I can inflict this wound?

Most people would probably agree that execution in such a case seems a bit excessive. Maybe he should just cut my tongue out—put that angel with the flaming sword back to work? Or maybe we expect God to be a bit more subtle than that. Maybe we'd just like him to flag me down, and suggest in that moment that what I'm about to do is terribly destructive, unloving, and morally wrong. Well, isn't that in fact what he does? We call that "having a conscience," and our whole legal system is built around the assumption that virtually every person has one, and knows the difference between right and wrong. Successful "insanity" pleas (which, depending on the state, mean either not knowing the difference or not being able to act on knowledge of the difference) are exceedingly rare—less than 1 percent of all cases tried in criminal court. Psychologists call those who either don't know the difference between right and wrong, or are indifferent to the difference and to the suffering of those they victimize, "sociopaths," and these, too, are exceedingly rare.

The vast majority of humans have a working conscience, though they vary in sensitivity, and this is apparently what God relies on to keep us from inflicting irreparable harm on each other in the heat of a marital spat or any other conflict. I've already suggested that this system doesn't work perfectly, that partners do wound each other, sometimes bitterly. But this brings us back to the issues of freedom and choice. Partners who treat each other well only because they are prevented from doing otherwise by angels with flaming swords cannot have a "loving" relationship in any meaningful sense. As a member of my parish put it, without freedom there can be no love, because without freedom one cannot give the gift of oneself.[6]

That's true for couples, and it's also true of our relationship with God: love must be chosen, not forced. The offering of our self must be a gift, not a tax. Evidently God designed human-kind not to be his colony or his slaves, but his household, his own beloved family. To bring that about, in his omnipotence he made himself outrageously vulnerable, issuing an invitation he gave us the freedom to reject. Some days I try to point out that although this reveals the magnitude of God's love, it does not necessarily reveal his sanity. He doesn't seem particularly troubled by this, and if as Lady Julian said, "all will be well, and all will be well, and all manner of thing will be well," then perhaps I can accept it too. Most days I can accept that God is crazy enough, and crazy enough about us, to think this whole experiment is worth the trouble. But accepting it doesn't mean I understand. I can dig around in the problem of evil, but when I dig deep enough to encounter God, I run into mystery. When that happens, I lay down my shovel and fall on my face at his feet. And when I see that those feet are wounded, I'm reminded that however little I understand about God's response to evil and suffering, I know for sure that he does not observe it from a safe distance. He has cared enough to enter into it completely, and bear the full weight of it in his own body and soul. And I find that, for now at least, that's answer enough for me.

Chapter Seven

Seeing in the Dark:
A Little Journal of
Unheroic Suffering

If [one] wishes to be sure of the road he travels on,
he must close his eyes and walk in the dark.

—Saint John of the Cross, *The Dark Night of the Soul*

My back has gone out again. This always seems to happen at the most inopportune times, typically when I'm far from home and there's no one to take care of me. I am one of nature's hermits, and although there are a few people in my life whose company I cherish, I also love, even crave, spells of solitude. Except when I'm sick or injured; then I become a complete baby and hate to be left alone.

There's no help for it at the moment, however, as I'm over four thousand miles from Seattle, living on my own in a little flat in Belfast, Northern Ireland, running a study abroad program on conflict and reconciliation. It's almost three weeks now since the initial injury, and things are starting to look up. But I've been touched over and over by how generously God has met my needs during this time: I got in right away to see a doctor who reassured me[1] and provided drugs that helped without putting me in a stupor. My landlord got me a brand-new mattress—and then another one, when that one wasn't firm enough. And I've been given the grace throughout to know I'm not really alone. When these back episodes get bad enough, I tend to feel like something catastrophic is about to happen, like any minute my body is going to snap in two. Yet even in my worst moments, I had to admit that I'd been given everything I really needed. God's grace was sufficient (2 Cor 12:9); every time I needed help, he came through.

But he didn't take away the pain. I joked that, since I was planning to get back to writing on suffering, God wanted me to do my fieldwork first. But of course, I don't imagine that God inflicted this on me; it was most likely the combination of a bad mattress and a marathon grading session where I sat at my table for hours without a break. I have chronic back trouble, so I ought to have known better than to sit for such a long time, but when it comes to backs, it only takes one careless act to get you in real trouble. So I'm going to be writing about suffering with some fresh personal experience, but my experience of suffering is completely banal and unheroic. I'm not in pain because I rescued a child from a burning building, or donated a kidney to a stranger, or insisted on the divinity of Christ. I'm in pain because I pretended for a few hours that I have a normal back.

So what I want to know is, does my pain have any meaning, or is it just a pointless waste? People often speak of suffering as "redemptive," as if our troubles have a larger meaning, some part to play in God's redeeming work in the world. But does this apply to all suffering? It's easy enough to grasp the meaning of suffering on behalf of others, or for one's convictions, but what about the pain we endure just because, as they say, "Shit happens"?

Thinking about the redemptive potential of suffering brings me to the other end of the spectrum, the most meaningful suffering of all: the Passion and death of Christ. At the moment,

I'm reading a novel based on the life of Jesus,[2] and as always, I was tempted to skip the account of the Passion. In fact, I recently read another Jesus novel,[3] and I'm sorry to say I skipped right from Palm Sunday to Easter. Passion narratives are a bit like spiritual PTSD: you get to relive the events in all their horror, and there's only so much emotional upheaval on that scale I can take. I recognize the tears and nausea for the graces they are, but sometimes there's only so much *grace* I can take.

Yes, I know how it ends. But on the way there, I'm face-to-face with a love I can't understand. I know I made this necessary, that I put Jesus in this position. I used to weep mostly about that; now my tears are less about me, and more about him. I'm outraged at the crime, sickened by the force of dark blows to his body and spirit, appalled by his willingness to absorb them all alone. The injustice and perversion, the sheer ugliness of it all exhausts me, and I demand to know why he thinks this is worthwhile. I tell him once again that he's crazy; he thanks me for my support. For one brief moment, I see myself redeemed: bright, clean, restored, along with countless others and the whole of creation. I still don't think it's worth it. The idea that it was worth all of this to become one with a human soul like mine, to walk once more in the garden with me in the cool of the day, is just nuts.

But apparently God is nuts, and really does desire union with my soul that much. And just when I think the Christian faith can't get any weirder, I notice something more curious still: for all my cowardice and dread of the smallest discomfort, there's a part of me that really wants to be on that cross with him. Christ's desire to be one with me took him the way of suffering, and in some strange symmetry, my oneness with him makes me want to suffer with him, to be completely identified with him in this, as in everything.

Maybe my oneness with him lies principally in the fact that now I'm crazy too. It probably looks that way. Some skeptics would talk about repressed guilt and a desire for punishment.

I did wrestle with feelings of guilt in the early years of my re-conversion, in that period known as "purgation," but God and I have moved on a bit since then. Others would point to the old and destructive tradition of Christian hyper-asceticism, see-ing self-imposed suffering as reflecting a pathologically dim view of human nature. But I share their horror of religiously induced masochism; this is not what I'm talking about. (Besides, no one who knows me would accuse me of asceticism.) Jesus never sought out suffering for its own sake, nor did his words or actions suggest that suffering was anything other than an evil to be eradicated.

To induce suffering in anyone, including ourselves, in the name of God is to take that name in vain—in short, it is blas-phemy. The desire to be on the cross with Jesus is, first, last, and always, the desire to be *with Jesus.* It is not a wish to hang on a cross for the hell of it, so to speak. It's the longing to be close to him wherever he is, knowing that the cross is one of those places. As his mother, Mary had loved Jesus longer and more fiercely than anyone. As she stood there watching her son's agony, I'm sure she would have traded places with him if she could; that's what mothers are like. She couldn't trade places with him, so she did the next best thing: she stayed there and agonized with him. And that is where I want to be.

There are other models as well: Francis of Assisi is said to have received the stigmata because he prayed to know intimately the suffering of Christ, as well as the love that drove him to it. Of course, Francis lived in a culture that celebrated the ideal of courtly love, and as we have seen, he understood suffering for love to be part of the great romantic adventure. This kind of romantic heroism doesn't fly so well in our day, when we are encouraged to find God in the ordinary, the little routines and small miracles of daily life. And so we should, but the two ap-proaches are not mutually exclusive; it's just that seeing the sig-nificance of the ordinary requires a bit of romantic imagination. Accusing Francis of overzealous romanticism is like shooting fish in a barrel, but if we're going to dismiss the stigmatized saint of Assisi, we'll also have to dump the more staid St. Paul, who "want[ed] to know Christ and the power of his resurrection *and the sharing of his sufferings* by becoming like him in his death" (Phil 3:10).[4]

Compassion: Sharing the Pain

Suffering is back in the news—not that it's ever far away, but this is suffering on a huge scale. The United Nations estimates that the cyclone that hit Burma two weeks ago has killed over 100,000 people, and affected 2.5 million.[5] The death toll from the earthquake in China one week ago is inching toward 50,000, with another 250,000 wounded and millions homeless.[6] A shockingly high percentage of the dead are children, buried under collapsed schools, and to add to the grief, some 200 rescue workers have been killed by mud slides. News footage shows streets covered with bodies, and pockets of grief-stricken parents. This being China, many of these parents lost their only child. There are going to be some hard questions put to those who built those schools, and the reporters are suggesting that some of them may answer with their lives.

I'm arguing with God again. This is getting to be a habit. But this time I'm not asking the reason for all this suffering; after all, we covered that in the last chapter. This time I want to know the meaning of this kind of suffering. Because really, the difference between these catastrophes and my back pain is not of type but of scale: obviously they differ in magnitude, and their suffering certainly makes mine seem puny and kind of embarrassing. But both these disasters and my back pain are examples of what I'm calling unheroic suffering: not the result of voluntary sacrifice, but mainly just drawing the short straw in a fallen world.

So what I want to know is this: is there any way in which my suffering can enable me, as St. Paul says, to share in the sufferings of Christ, and become like him in his death? Is there some opportunity here for solidarity with him, and with the suffering millions in Burma and China? Can a small case of back pain make a bridge from me to God, to my neighbor? In the King James Version, the verse from Philippians that speaks of "the sharing of his suffering" is rendered "the fellowship of his suffering." Is there some way in which my suffering brings me into fellowship with others who suffer, including Christ?

The first thing to do is to get over being apologetic about the issue of magnitude. Again, a sense of perspective, and a respect for the differences between levels of pain, is important. I'm pretty sure that Jesus, the master storyteller, loves the story of the princess and the pea. But there is something also to be learned from the similarities between my large and small examples of suffering. So let's just accept that unheroic suffering comes in all sizes, and ask, in what sense can this kind of suffering be *redemptive*?

Since "redemptive suffering" is essentially a Catholic idea, I figured I might as well start at the top. In his apostolic letter *Salvifici Doloris*, On the Christian Meaning of Suffering, Pope John Paul II wrote:

> Every man has *his own share in the Redemption*. Each one is also *called to share in that suffering* through which the Redemption was accomplished. He is called to share in that suffering through which all human suffering has also been redeemed. In bringing about the Redemption through suffering, Christ *has* also *raised human suffering to the level of the Redemption*. Thus each man, in his suffering, can also become a sharer in the redemptive suffering of Christ.[7]

I find these words encouraging, but not particularly instructive. That is, I sense that there is a deep truth here, but I don't have any more clarity on it than I did before. Most Catholics I've heard talk about redemptive suffering link it to a longstanding tradition of "offering up" personal afflictions of even the most mundane kind for the spiritual welfare of others. Elaine M. Prevallet, SL, describes the understanding of this practice that she grew up with:

> As children, we learned the phrase as something like a religious version of "grin and bear it." For me, it meant that if I "made a sacrifice" of my own preference, and put that sacrifice in God's hands, I could somehow "get some grace" for myself or for someone else who needed it, like the "souls in purgatory."[8]

Let me say that I firmly believe in purgatory: I think we're all going to have to face up to the truth about ourselves and our lives before we're fit for celestial company, and for most of us that's going to be somewhat painful. Those who are going through that process are probably in need of our prayers; I don't see that as different from praying for those whose struggles continue on earth. And "offering it up" has the advantage of using any and every kind of suffering for the sake of others. Life doesn't have to give us the opportunity to rescue a drowning stranger; if I drop the blender on my foot, I can turn that pain toward the benefit of others.

But I still can't understand why that should be. I just can't make the connection between my suffering something like back pain and the well-being of souls in this life or the next. And if I can't make the connection, for me at least the whole thing is in danger of descending into magic, almost like rubbing a lamp and waiting for the genie to emerge. As much as I believe in the communion of saints, I also believe we're all going to have to work out our own salvation,[9] and I don't see how my suffering can be used to feed someone else's meter.

And yet, I'm haunted by this idea that suffering can be redemptive. In his letter to the Colossians (1:24), St. Paul makes a breathtakingly audacious statement: "I am now rejoicing in my sufferings for your sake, and in my flesh I am completing what is lacking in Christ's afflictions for the sake of his body, that is, the church." There is a suggestion here that, as his Body remaining in the world, disciples are invited to participate with

Christ somehow in his work of redemption, and that this work involves suffering. Indeed, Scripture is full of assurances that joining in the work of Christ will involve suffering, from Jesus' blessing on those who are persecuted for righteousness's sake (Matt 5:10-11) to Paul's statement to Timothy that "all who want to live a godly life in Christ Jesus will be persecuted" (2 Tim 3:12).

But most of these passages are concerned with suffering in the line of duty, that is, persecution for the faith. It's sort of like workers' comp, where it only "counts" if you get hurt on the job. An exception is Jesus' assertion (Luke 9:23) that following him means denying oneself and taking up the cross. Since he doesn't specify what form that cross might take, there's room here to see it as any kind of suffering, and Christians have mostly given it this broad interpretation. But it seems to me that the passages that most strongly suggest that suffering somehow links us intimately to Christ in his Passion and death are those (like 2 Cor 4:8-11)[10] that refer to suffering directly in the cause of the gospel. That leaves other, less heroic forms of suffering looking kind of barren.

Of course, God has a long history of bringing fruit from that which looks barren; wombs that are too old, wombs that are too new, nothing seems to faze him when he wants to bring something to birth. My unheroic suffering feels like a kind of infertility, and I'm inclined, like Sarah of old, to take the promise of fruitfulness as a joke. Sarah was wrong, and I suspect I am too. But like her, I just can't quite see how this is going to happen. I'm tying myself into knots in the dark, and at this point all I can see are my own intellectual limits, which are too depressingly clear. I'm pushing against mystery here, and it's pushing right back.

Night Vision

My condition has taken a turn for the worse, and suddenly my questions about the meaning of suffering seem like a pointless academic exercise. I'm not interested in amateur theologizing now; I'm scared. Yesterday my pain forced me to the emergency room at Belfast City Hospital, where I stood for two hours, waiting to be seen on a holiday weekend and unable to sit down for fear of making it worse. The ER doctor said that, contrary to the reassuring diagnosis of the doctor I saw earlier, this is certainly a herniated disc rather than simple muscular inflammation. That's more serious, though not in itself catastrophic. What would be catastrophic is if the herniation is pointing toward the center of the spine, rather than off to the side. This would put me at risk of "cauda equina syndrome,"[11] a surgical emergency where compression of the nerves in the lower part of the spinal canal can produce permanent paralysis of the legs and loss of bladder and bowel control. The fact that I'm feeling pins and needles in both legs rather than just one side has the doctor looking concerned.

I can't know for sure how serious my situation is without an MRI, and the ER doctor tells me that the National Health Service wouldn't consider my symptoms grave enough to order that right away. But since I'm supposed to leave in a week and lead my husband and two friends all over Europe, I sort of need to know right now if I'm on the verge of a spinal emergency. So it looks like, once the weekend is over, I can probably pay about a thousand dollars and get a private clinic to do it. Then maybe they'll administer an epidural steroid injection that will see me through the three weeks of travel ahead. I'm all for it. But Tuesday is two days away.

So once again I've gone spiritually primal. I'm still over four thousand miles from home, husband, and all that's comforting. At this point I don't care about the meaning of my suffering; I just want it to stop. I want someone to tell me I'll be okay, that I'm not going to suddenly lose control of bodily functions and have to be rushed into surgery, that I'm not even going to have to cancel my friends' dream vacation in Europe, that I won't have to be responsible for all of us losing a lot of money.

But mostly I want to know that I'm not going to have to call an ambulance and figure out a way for the paramedics to get into this secure building in time to keep me from becoming paralyzed.

"Look to your faith," my husband says, a faith he doesn't altogether share, but he respects its power. I tell him that if it weren't for that faith, I'd have sunk into despair a long time ago. So yes, it helps, but it's not that simple. God has a tendency to disappear at times like this, if he thinks you can take it. It's what Jesus experienced: *why have you forsaken me?* How could Jesus lose touch with the Father at the precise moment when he most needed him? A lot of people think of religion as a crutch,[12] and assume that it's a great comfort in times of need, but in Jesus' greatest need, he felt totally alone. I think religion is less like a crutch, and more like a skateboard: sometimes it carries us, but other times we carry it instead, and it can be pretty heavy. A friend suggests that mine is more like a canoe, and I'm on a long portage.

God knows it's long. Another full day before I can even try to get a referral to a private clinic. There are moments when time seems to stop, and it's just me, God, and my fear. And the worst of it is that I can't really seem to find God, so mostly it's just me and my fear. Belfast has always been a "thin place" for me, where God is vividly present, more real to me than the people around me. This visit has been no exception, and the days and weeks since I arrived have been filled with intense prayer: intimate conversation and the quiet security of a shared pulse.

But in the three days since this crisis began, all that has disappeared, along with God. I try to pray, but I'm too agitated to listen. I try music, which is usually able to cut through any distractions; it sounds like random noise. British television is not exactly effective at taking my mind off it, since of the four channels, three seem to be showing sports I don't understand and the other will be a Schwarzenegger movie or an Australian soap. So I just lie here feeling my symptoms, my loneliness, and my fear. A week ago my prayer was deeply satisfying; now when I can pray at all, I can only croak out inarticulate cries for help. I borrow words from those who have them: "Save me, oh God, for the waters are come in unto my soul" (Ps 69:1). No response. I'm going to bed, but before I do, I make sure there are three things on my nightstand: my cell phone, my address, and my keys, so I can throw them down to the paramedics if necessary.

❖   ❖   ❖

Sleep: God's gift to those who suffer. An escape, an oasis in a desert of anxiety and pain. I was really enjoying being unconscious, but at precisely 5:42 a.m. a couple of guys started a spirited conversation directly under my bedroom window. So I figured, if I can't sleep, I might as well see if God's back. I shut the window, go back to bed, and try to pray.

And there he is, filling me with peace. It's like a sensation remembered from long ago, but in fact it's only been a few days. He will be with me, and all will be well. I'm nervously aware that to God, disability and death are not incompatible with all being well, but I'm taking what I can get. And I'm understanding something: if God has let everything go dim on me, it's because he knows there are some things I can see best in the dark. This is an altogether different form of sightseeing from what I was planning, but then, I agree with whoever it was who said our plans mainly exist to give God a laugh. So what have I seen so far on my little nighttime tour; has this experience taught me anything about suffering? I know that suffering can teach us patience, can make us compassionate, can give us the ability to comfort others in their distress. But my question has been very specific: how can my involuntary, unheroic suffering unite me to Christ and his work of redemption?

The first thing I saw was that because I am already united to Christ as part of his Body, I cannot suffer apart from him, nor he from me. This is true no matter what form suffering may take. Saint Paul claimed that he was "completing what is lacking in Christ's afflictions for the sake of his body, that is, the church" (Col 1:24). Obviously Christ's afflictions were complete when Paul wrote this, both in the sense that they ended with his death and that they were entirely sufficient for the work of redemption, and need no supplementation from the likes of us. And yet, when Jesus appeared to Saul on the road to Damascus, he did not ask, "Why are you persecuting my church?" but "Why are you persecuting *me*?" The church is his Body on earth. Nothing but death could separate him from his Body, and Christ has overcome death. So he and his Body are joined forever, and any pain that afflicts the one will of necessity be shared by the other: "If one member suffers, all suffer together with it" (1 Cor 12:26). They must experience it as one.

The letter to the Ephesians (5:25-30) says that no man ever hates his own body (notice it doesn't say that no *woman* does). He may or may not admire it, but either way he feeds it, attentively cares for it, and feels whatever pain goes on in it. This, the author insists, is how a man must relate to his wife. Then the whole analysis is extended to, in the words of the *Book of Common Prayer*, "the mystery of the union between Christ and his church."[13] The church is the bride of Christ, and in marriage, spouses become "one flesh." It is impossible for one to remain unaffected while the other suffers. If I may throw in a further comparison, one spouse can no more be indifferent to the other's suffering than one part of a baseball team can win while the other loses. They are in it together.

I'm finally beginning to get this, not as an academic exercise, but as lived experience. It's not the suffering that makes us one; our baptism has done that. But the fact that we are already one means that we suffer as one—one with Christ himself, and one with the rest of his Body. One thing I've noticed lately is that my thoughts and prayers increasingly turn toward others who are suffering: the sick, the poor, prisoners, refugees, those who have no voice, those who are alone. Intercessory prayer is not my strong point; I don't do it very much or very well. But since this struggle with my back began, I notice that even my guilty awareness that others suffer more than I do turns my thoughts regularly to them, and to the vulnerability that we share in our common humanity. Increasingly I find that the prayer that starts as "God help me" mysteriously shifts into "God help *them*," and finishes as "God help *us*." If one member suffers, all suffer together with it. Perhaps there is a part for me in the work of redemption after all, and my pain is showing me the way.

Further, the fellowship of our shared suffering, Paul suggests, effects a spiritual transformation in us: we become "like him in his death." If, in my suffering, I am open to this kind of trans-formation, to drawing closer to Christ by becoming more like him, then I can hardly see that suffering as wasted. God does not give us pain but he will, with sadness, use such pain as comes our way to continue our conversion. I believe that God hates it when we suffer; he despises our pain and wants it to end, longs to comfort us and would not tolerate it unless it served a larger purpose.

That brings me to the second thing I saw on my nighttime excursion: in this case, at least, I had given my consent to this "larger purpose." I wanted to know him, and the fellowship of his suffering. I wanted to be one with him on the cross, to share a bond of solidarity with those who suffer, in short, to love God and my neighbor from close-up, to be *involved*. I wanted to be able to say something about suffering, not from a safe distance; that is not God's way. Wounded healers can speak to suffering because they know it from inside, and now I know it a little better too.[14]

In saying I gave my consent to this suffering, I mean that in certain rash moments, I have handed God a blank check. You know the kind of thing I mean: those prayers that end with ". . . whatever it takes." I've noticed that God has a disturbing tendency to take those kinds of requests seriously, perhaps more seriously than we meant them. And we don't always recognize the answers to those prayers for what they are. Brennan Manning has pointed out that we often say things like, "Lord, give me humility," and then when a humiliating failure comes our way, we wonder why God has abandoned us, when in reality he's just granted our prayer. What if God had actually said to me, "Well, how about this as a plan: You go off to a foreign country away from your friends and family and have an injury that leaves you at risk of paralysis, and try to run a program while dealing with pain and a rising sense of panic. Oh, and by the way, when you're most afraid, I'll be out of reach." I am a coward at heart, and had I known the details, I'm pretty sure I would have wormed my way out of it somehow.

But I had consented to suffering, and once it began I didn't have the power to make it stop. So I figured I might as well trust God to see me through, reminding myself of St. Peter in one of his less admirable moments. Jesus has just preached a controversial sermon, inviting his audience to consume his flesh and blood (John 6). This was a pretty outrageous thing to say to a congregation of Jews, for whom cannibalism was an unthinkable taboo. Jesus couldn't have been surprised, though he was certainly disappointed, when even many of his disciples walked out on him. Turning to the Twelve, he asked if they intended to leave too, and Peter, in a spectacular demonstration of loyalty, indicated that they would stay because they had nowhere else to go.[15]

One thing I love about God is how he accepts even the shabbiest gifts from us. This brings me to the third thing I discovered on my nighttime tour, namely, the depth of my own poverty. In keeping with the medieval courtly myth, I'm inclined to think that talk is cheap, and am suspicious of declarations of love that are never backed up by sacrifices. Indeed, as a lay Franciscan, I have vowed to uphold the principle that "love is measured by sacrifice."[16] I wanted to offer God a big, pricey love, and I wanted to prove that love by giving God something that cost me. I once heard that a committee questioning prospective bishops in the Episcopal Church asked each candidate the question, "What have you risked for the gospel?" That question resonates with me, because I want my commitment to be more than talk, and costly gifts do make a point.

But in my suffering, and especially in my cowardly response to my suffering, I realized that I don't have the resources to offer big, impressive gifts to God. And that is God's costly gift to *me* in this experience, the hard lesson that hurt him too. As Elaine Prevallet puts it,

> I believe the crux of the mystery of suffering is the tension in every human life between control and vulnerability. Suffering, more than any other human experience, has the capacity to subvert our ingrained illusion that we control the course of events in our lives. Suffering challenges our idol of self-sufficiency, inviting us to realize that we are not now—and never were—calling the shots.[17]

The Franciscan way points to the self-emptying poverty and humility of Christ, and asks us to emulate it. As a middle-class professional in the wealthy First World, I have struggled with how to reconcile my comfortable standard of living with this call of the gospel.[18] But I'm learning that there are many forms of wealth, and just as many forms of poverty. Perhaps you could say that any stripping away of our illusions of self-sufficiency, and the consequent realization of our dependence on God, is "poverty," just as real a poverty as being chronically broke.

I'm coming to see this poverty for the gift it is. Every kind of suffering, including wounds of body and soul, creates empty, negative space within us, and negative space tends to draw God in. Fasting operates on this principle: it's the voluntary creation of negative space within us, to make room for God. There's a kind of spiritual vacuum effect here, but not because we have to tug on God to bring him close. He already desires to be close to us; it's just that we continually plug that space with noise, company, amusements, and consumption of every kind, so that we never have to see how poor we really are. The Laodiceans were like that, and Jesus had some harsh words for them: "you say, 'I am rich, I have prospered, and I need nothing.' You do not realize that you are wretched, pitiable, poor, blind, and naked" (Rev 3:17). With those who know they are poor, though, he is tender in his blessing, and promises them the kingdom of heaven (Matt 5:3; Luke 6:20).

❖   ❖   ❖

I got the epidural, by the mercy of God, and it saw me through the three weeks of travel and the long flight home. I had dreaded that flight for a couple of months, but at every point on the journey, God was there with a gift. It turned out to be, if not painless, at least not the traumatic experience I'd feared. I got to enjoy a week of being home before I relapsed, then began another round of tests and visits to doctors and physical therapists. As I write this, I've been mostly confined to quarters for a month, the pain coming and going, the blues coming and going with it. Since I can't do much, the days are pretty long. My husband and my sister have both been out of town for the past week, which has increased my loneliness. It's all starting to feel pretty bleak, as if the whole world has contracted into a seedy little bus station: gray, grim, and mostly deserted, with nothing much to do but keep an eye on the sketchy figures that occasionally drift through. And the journey ahead is nothing to look forward to.

And yet, I managed to make it to church a couple of Sundays ago, and a funny thing happened.[19] We heard the story of how the patriarch Jacob was on the run after swindling his brother Esau out of his birthright. One night Jacob lay down to sleep, and dreamed of a ladder between earth and heaven, with the angels of God ascending and descending on it. Disgraceful as Jacob's behavior had been, he at least recognized the Holy when he saw it, and declared: "Surely the LORD is in this place—and I did not know it!" (Gen 28:16). And then, as if God didn't quite trust me to get the point, we had Psalm 139:

> Whither shall I go from thy spirit? Or whither shall I flee from thy presence?
> If I ascend up into heaven, thou art there: if I make my bed in hell, behold, thou art there.
> If I take the wings of the morning, and dwell in the uttermost parts of the sea;
> Even there shall thy hand lead me, and thy right hand shall hold me.
> If I say, Surely the darkness shall cover me; even the night shall be light about me.
> Yea, the darkness hideth not from thee; but the night shineth as the day: the darkness and the light are both alike to thee.[20]

It seems to me that the greatest truths of the spiritual life are found in paradoxes. "If I make my bed in hell, thou art there." But there can be no hell where God is; the presence of God is heaven, by definition. So even hell is heaven, if we can only see it, and if I made my bed in heaven, and he were not there, it would be hell to me. Meditating on the incarnation, on the coming of God-with-us, John's gospel says, "The light shines in the darkness" (John 1:5). The verse goes on to say, "and the darkness did not overcome it." It doesn't say that the darkness went away because the light was shining; it says that the light shines *in the darkness.* God is in the very darkness itself; darkness is a living thing, alive and holy, suffused with God. And when night closes in around me, if I'm paying attention, I can experience that darkness as an embrace.

Surely the Lord is in my bus station, and I did not know it. But if that is where Jesus awaits me at this moment, then that is where I want to be. A dear friend who's an atheist asked me recently what it feels like when I'm aware of the presence of God. I told her about Julian of Norwich, the fourteenth-century

English mystic, who is thought to have been the first woman to write a book in the English language. Lady Julian is best known for her line, "And all will be well, and all will be well, and all manner of thing will be well." I told my friend that when I'm most aware of God's presence, I feel a deep inner certainty of the truth of that statement. "Well, then, what does it feel like when God seems absent?" That took a bit more thought, but my best answer is that I know, rather than feel, the truth of Julian's words. If I close my eyes, I know the furniture in this room is still here, though my senses offer me no reassurance. And if life pulls the shades down on me for a while, I know God is still here.

I want to be well. I'm praying and working toward that goal. My physical therapist is kicking my butt; that's what physical therapists do. PT is a bit like boot camp, but I know these sadistic bullies are just trying to keep us in one piece. So I'm working on healing, but until it comes, I'm consenting to pass the time with Jesus in this tough place. The pain, the boredom, and the blues are still with me. But at least my night vision is a little better now. I've struggled to find meaning in my suffering, and I've learned that, although there's nothing inherently noble in a back injury, any suffering can be ennobled by the presence of Christ. Indeed, even the most heroic suffering cannot be ennobled without it: "If I give all my possessions to feed the poor, and if I surrender my body to be burned, but do not have love, it profits me nothing" (1 Cor 13:3 NASB).

Most importantly, though, I've seen once again that God never leads us into the dark to abandon us, but only to draw us closer. So we can rail against the darkness, fight against our poverty, plug the negative space within us, and try to maintain the illusion of self-sufficiency and control. We can make our bed in hell, and try to get comfortable there. Or we can surrender ourselves with joy, and enter into a deeper intimacy with Christ, one with him and each other in his suffering and in his triumph. Meister Eckhart said, "The fastest beast that will carry you to your perfection is suffering."[21] The beast has bolted, and I'm not much of a rider. But I like the destination, and I'm hanging on.

Chapter Eight

Midnight in the Desert

> O my brother, the contemplative is the man not who has fiery visions of the cherubim carrying God on their imagined chariot, but simply he who has risked his mind in the desert.
>
> —Thomas Merton, *I Have Seen What I Was Looking For: Selected Spiritual Writings*, ed. M. Basil Pennington

Relationships are so predictable, aren't they? I have a friend who is currently embarking on a new relationship, and last night he was telling me rather more than I felt entitled to know about how much he's enjoying this stage. At a certain point, however, he paused and acknowledged that the novelty phase never lasts, and what do you do then?

That's one of the big questions of the spiritual life, isn't it? Our relationship with God, like our romantic relationships (and, as Ronald Rolheiser has pointed out,[1] even our relationships with friends, our vocations, pet causes, and so on), is U-shaped. It starts out on a big high, where every encounter is thrilling and fulfilling, and every direction you look there's a glimpse of heaven. Prayer is exciting, church is the high point of the week, and we really, really *understand* what Jesus meant when he said he wanted our joy to be full.

But eventually, inevitably, the excitement dies down. The change may be as subtle as noticing that I'm checking my watch in church, or it may be a crushing disillusionment when the Body of Christ proves all too human. Or it could be some other loss or blow—unemployment, illness, grief, a back injury, even—and God chooses that moment to disappear. Like romantic relationships, our spiritual life can be riddled with conflict and confusion, or just grow boring and stale. Either way, the shine is off the penny, and that joy Jesus talked about sounds like the kind of youthful enthusiasm that jaded adults tend to dismiss as naïveté.

So we wonder what to do, how to rekindle the flame. The problem is that while most of us know how it feels to fall in love, we don't really know how to bring the condition about. This is why we represent it as being struck by an arrow: falling in love is the sort of thing that just hits us while we're minding our own business, and our role is to be passive, unwitting targets. I have no data to prove it, but I would guess that suicide by arrow is pretty rare. And while I've seen plenty of sentimental images of people struck helplessly in love by Cupid's magic dart, I can't recall ever seeing anyone take an arrow that's fallen out, and put it back in again. We just don't know how to do that. And because we don't, when we hit the bottom of the U and the delight disappears, we tend to panic, and we often misinterpret what's happening.

Maybe I've sinned. Probably I've sinned, even if I can't figure out how. Or I'm just generally inadequate: God's got an inner circle, and I didn't make the cut. Or else, it's God's fault: I did everything I was supposed to do (does anyone actually believe this?), and where is he? In other words, when things go wrong, our instinct is to figure someone's at fault. And whether we point the finger at ourselves or God, either way we feel abandoned. In time, if nothing changes, we may become resigned to a joyless relationship, or we may start looking for a way out.

This is a mistake, though, because good relationships are U-shaped, not L-shaped, and the temptation to give up too early can rob us of the most rewarding part. As I explained to my friend, if you stick it out through the low part, there is an upswing eventually. A lesson I learned from Rolheiser is that at the beginning of a love relationship, during the infatuation period, what I really love about the other person is how he makes *me* feel, what he does for me. It's not until you've stuck with the other through the rocky parts that you know that your love and commitment (and the other's) are real. When you reach that point, the relationship may lack some of the excitement of novelty, but what you get in return is something much richer and more profound.

This chapter is about the bottom of the U, the times when there's no delight in sight. We'll look at the ways we try to make sense of spiritual darkness and aridity when they descend on us, and what God is up to in this part of our journey. In the last two chapters I've approached suffering from a more theological perspective: why does God allow evil to exist, and in what sense can suffering be "redemptive"? Here I want to take a more experiential approach, and see suffering—especially spiritual suffering—as *formative*, that is, as crucial to the shaping of our souls.

From the earliest days of the Christian faith, writers have grappled with these issues, trying to come to terms with the sense of God's absence, the desolation it brings, and how these experiences bring us to a deeper, more intimate knowledge of God. In their work I find three images particularly resonant: the desert, the gift of tears, and darkness. These images can bring us to a better understanding of how the form of the U itself forms us, and readies us for the soul-shaking experience of union with God. If "no eye has seen, nor ear heard, nor the human heart conceived, what God has prepared for those who love him" (1 Cor 2:9)—if, that is, we cannot begin to imagine what God has in store for us, it stands to reason that we're going to have to be prepared for it. We're going to have to change somehow. I am going to try to show that the scary place at the bottom of the U is a critical part of that preparation, and, paradoxical as it seems, a sign of God's limitless love for us.

The Desert

The powerful image of the desert (and, equally, of "wilderness") is part of the rich symbolic legacy Christians inherited from Judaism. For obvious historical and geographic reasons, the desert had a special significance in the ancient Hebrew mind. But what is striking about desert imagery is its multivalent character, that is, its ability to evoke multiple meanings. Like passion, the desert has two faces. On the one hand, the desert represents the absence of God: a place of exile, of wandering lost, a place to which the scapegoat, bearing the sins of the people, was sent to die (Lev 16:21). Hebrew has multiple words for "desert," as you might expect, conveying ideas such as aridity, desolation, hostility to human life. In the Septuagint,[2] the Greek word *éremos*, from which our word *hermit* is derived, picks up this notion of desolation and loneliness, and was translated into the Latin of the Vulgate as *desolatio* or *solitudo*.[3] This is the frightening face of the desert: a place of abandonment, of forsakenness, where there is no place to hide and all paths disappear into the sand.

But there is another side to desert imagery. The children of Israel had forty tough years in the desert, but they also traveled in the very presence of God: the cloud by day, the fire by night, nourished on bread from heaven and water from the rock. If the desert was a forbidding place where scapegoats and servants were sent to die (Gen 20:8-20), it was also the place where Moses met God and received the law that would make Israel holy. Later, the wilderness becomes the place where God will draw all of Israel into intimacy with himself:

> Therefore, I will now allure her,
>   and bring her into the wilderness,
>   and speak tenderly to her.
> From there I will give her her vineyards,
>   and make the Valley of Achor a door of hope.
> There she shall respond as in the days of her youth,
>   as at the time when she came out of the land of Egypt.

> On that day, says the LORD, you will call me, "My husband,"
> and no longer will you call me, "My Baal [Master]." . . . And
> I will take you for my wife forever; I will take you for my wife
> in righteousness and in justice, in steadfast love, and in mercy.
> I will take you for my wife in faithfulness; and you shall know
> the LORD. (Hos 2:14-16, 19-20)

Notice that the Hebrew word translated here as "know" ("you
shall *know* the Lord") does not refer just to "head" knowledge;
it refers to mental, spiritual, and emotional engagement. It carries a connotation of intimacy, of affection, even of sexual union[4]
("Now the man [Adam] *knew* his wife Eve, and she conceived
and bore Cain"[5]). God wanted Israel to know him "in the
biblical sense," and he would lead her out into the desert, not
to abandon her but to woo her, to draw her back into loving
relationship with himself. The U dips down, and swings up
again.

For Christians, the desert is the place where John the Baptist
preached, where Jesus was baptized and identified as the Beloved
Son, where he was tempted, and, significantly, where he re-
treated periodically to pray.[6] Jesus faced down the devil in the
desert, but he was also looked after there by angels (Matt 4:11).
It was in remote, isolated places where he sought the company
of his Father, and where he revealed himself most fully to his
friends. Jesus certainly experienced the austerities of the desert,
yet he sought it out again and again, precisely when his soul
needed refreshing.

After his baptism, we read that Jesus was led by the Spirit into
the wilderness, although I like the language in Mark's gospel
where the Spirit "drives" him out. I confess that my imagination
is not equal to the task of picturing what that looked like,[7] but
I do know what it's like when the Spirit drives me into the
desert: it looks like death, and I don't want to go. In his book
Soul Wilderness: A Desert Spirituality,[8] Kerry Walters gives us a
pretty good idea of what the desert experience looks like. He
explores the four stages of the spiritual journey identified by

Joseph Campbell, the heroic quest undertaken by those who hear the invitation to a deeper knowledge of God. The adventure begins with the call to leave home, the "driving into the wilderness." This tends to take the form of a growing discomfort with the status quo, until it becomes unbearable. Most of us prefer to remain in our comfort zone, and will only leave if forced ("driven") out.

Alan Jones[9] refers to this as "stopping the world," which is the extreme sense of internal dislocation we experience when the old ways of thinking, believing, and behaving don't work anymore. Something within us cracks open, and can't be patched up again. We can be brought to this point by a catastrophic event, or just a rising sense of unease that finally becomes intolerable:

> Our world suddenly stops and our old sense of who we are begins to fade. There is a moment of panic; but we wait, and a new way of knowing ourselves and the world begins to appear. This way of knowing does not give us control and power over things. It is not "useful" knowledge for the purpose of power and manipulation. We are introduced to a way of *un*knowing that is liberating, if frightening at first.[10]

The call to leave home can be terrifying, because we sense that the things we thought we knew—the world, God, our lives, our very selves—are all up for question; all our accustomed paths are about to be covered with sand. To be sure, some people are coaxed gently into the desert, while others are drawn by a flash of illumination. But most people are driven there by spiritual suffocation, when "home" becomes an airless labyrinth from which we must escape. The choice is stark, and no compromises are offered: "Either suffocate in the labyrinth or hurtle into the abyss."[11]

So we leave home, and that's when the discomforts really begin. Stage two of the quest takes us into the desert, where we're caught up in an epic battle in which everything we've held dear is at stake. The bad news is that we have no weapons, and we're going to lose. The good news is that this was the whole point all along. We go to the desert to die—to our false selves and our false gods, including our false images of the real God. We go there to be stripped of our illusions and introduced to the reality of our complete poverty. Any fantasies we entertained about our spiritual accomplishments, and all our plans for heroic service for God, disappear into the dust. The desert strips us naked, and we are ashamed.

What do these deserts look like? The desert tradition in Christianity really got underway after the Edict of Milan (313 CE) made the once outlawed faith legal throughout the Roman Empire. The willingness to suffer martyrdom had always been a mark of serious commitment to the faith, but when Christianity became first legal, then dominant, serious believers had to rethink what it meant to take up the cross and follow Jesus. Some of them found their answer in a life of extreme asceticism in the Egyptian desert, where they established a way of life based on renunciation and self-denial. The Desert Fathers and Mothers experimented with various forms: some lived as hermits, others in communities that were the forerunners of monasticism, others somewhere in between. In all cases, though, they sought a new kind of martyrdom, a "living" martyrdom; they trusted the desert to bring that about, and it did not disappoint them.[12]

But what about us? We have the same problems: the church is still a pretty comfortable and relatively unchallenging place to be (unless you're the wrong color, wrong sexual orientation, or a prophet or something), and an authentic Christian life still requires renunciation and sacrifice. But I don't see a movement of believers out to the desert in our day. A couple of friends just went to Las Vegas, but from what I heard the experience doesn't seem to have been a particularly ascetic one. During the school year, I can't manage so much as a weekend in Spokane, much less an extended sojourn in the desert, and in the summer I'm not going out there without air conditioning and a good sized pool.

Fortunately, the desert, like our Lord himself, comes to us in all kinds of guises. David Rensberger's insightful essay "Deserted Spaces" provides a catalogue of places where we can find ourselves isolated and alone, each one a "metaphorical . . . or virtual desert."[13] There are emotional deserts, like the marriage in which we feel alone, misunderstood, belittled, or unloved. The body can be a desert when disease, disability, or just old age strikes. Others may sympathize and help, but they cannot live there with us, nor can they die with us when the time comes. There are deserts of time and money: too little, too much, too little control over what we do have. There are vocational deserts: stuck in a job that no longer feels right, or perhaps never did, we may long to make a change but be unable to find a path. Of course, no job at all can be a particularly cruel and lonely desert. But any aspect of our life can become a desert; all that's required is an increasing sense of discomfort and loneliness in a situation that others can neither share nor fully understand.

Only a fool would go into the desert willingly, though of course all the saints, famous and obscure, have been holy fools at some level. But even if we come to the desert unwillingly, once there we can give our consent to its work on us. *This is where the two faces of passion merge into one*: our desire, our urgent need to be one with God, drives us to seek holiness "at any cost," even if it means dying alone under a hot sun. The poetry of the Beguines bears witness to the turbulent nature of the desert quest, and the motivation for it. Indeed, as Saskia Murk-Jansen shows,[14] the desert is a recurring theme in Beguine texts. This is Hadewijch:

> It is an incomprehensible wonder
> That has bound my heart
> And causes [me] to wander in a wild wilderness;
> Such a cruel desert was never created
> As love can make in her country

> Because she causes [us] to long for her with desire
> And to taste her being without knowledge.[15]

Sometimes it is our longing itself that propels us into the desert. In spite of all our reservations and what seems like our better judgment, we sense a call, and so we go. Yet even if we set out with enthusiasm, it's not easy to stay for the full treatment, and once out there, we'll do anything to avoid the death for which we came. There are all kinds of ways of weaseling out of this death. Some of us would rather baptize the false self than crucify it, so we lay a nice religious veneer over a fundamentally unsound structure, practicing a hollow conventional piety while we avoid a real encounter with this strange desert God.[16] Others simply drown out the summoning voice with busyness and distractions, anaesthetizing themselves with drink, drugs, career, shopping, TV, or whatever else is close at hand.

Still others seek refuge in rationality, in science and the illusion of control it brings. When Jacob Marley's ghost returns to his old partner Ebenezer Scrooge in *A Christmas Carol*, and warns him to change his ways, Scrooge tries to fight the specter off with reason, arguing that the apparition is just a product of bad digestion: "You may be an undigested bit of beef, a blot of mustard, a crumb of cheese, a fragment of an underdone potato. There's more of gravy than of grave about you, whatever you are!"[17] As Walters points out,[18] however, the desert is a koan, a paradox that has no "answers," only "responses." A koan is a riddle that a Zen master gives to the disciple, which defies resolution through the intellect ("What is the sound of one hand clapping?"). The disciple will meditate on the koan until thinking finally proves futile, and is discarded in favor of experience. At this point, when the arrogance of intellect is finally abandoned, the disciple achieves enlightenment.

If getting to this point were easy, there'd be a lot more enlightened people around, and we wouldn't have to pass laws against sending text messages while driving. But our tendency, when faced with an unsolvable puzzle, is to give up and turn our attention elsewhere. This is why some of the best counsel to come out of the ancient desert tradition was Abba Moses' advice to "Go, sit in your cell, and your cell will teach you everything."[19] Once we've left home and fled to the desert, the desert teaches us its greatest lesson, which is this: "Stop running. Stay where you are. Consent to feel what you feel—the loneliness, disorientation and terror—and stop trying to escape it." But as we have seen, escape is mighty tempting when acedia sets in:

> We are easily persuaded that the problem of growing up in the life of the spirit can be localized—*outside* ourselves. Somewhere else I could be nicer, holier, more balanced, more detached about criticism, more disciplined, able to sing in tune and probably thinner as well.[20]

How effective we could be, how brilliantly we could serve God someplace else, in a different job, a different parish, another ministry, another marriage. It's a mirage, though, because no matter where we go, as long as the problem is *inside* ourselves, we will continue to see the same imaginary oasis, tantalizingly out of reach.

We will not reach enlightenment, we will not learn the lesson of the desert or be ready to leave it, until we stop running and sit in our cell, alone with our poverty and that stern companion St. Francis called "Sister Death." As long as we think we have some resources, as long as we cling to the illusion that we might get out of here alive, the work of the desert is unfinished. But when we come to the end of ourselves, when the desert has stripped away every rag and shred with which we tried to cover ourselves and we have no covering and no place to hide, only then are we ready to enter the third stage of the quest, where "I will take you for my wife forever; I will take you for my wife in righteousness and in justice, in steadfast love, and in mercy. I will take you for my wife in faithfulness; and you shall know the Lord."

The third stage is where we discover that this seemingly empty, lonely desert is, in reality, filled with God. And if God has allowed the desert to strip us naked, it's because . . . well, he likes us that way. In Joseph Campbell's vision of the quest, this is the place where the soul comes to dwell with God. It is the place of union, of joyful consummation, the place where death gives way to resurrection. It is not, however, the final stage of the journey. Once this transformation has taken place and the soul is reanimated with the life of Christ, the hero must return home:

> The person who has arrived at her destiny may long to remain forever in the desert of whirling wings and divine silence. But she realizes that the wilderness transformation has named her a prophet, an emissary of God . . . So she turns back to the every-day world of noisy distraction, the realm of false selves and leering demons, to share with others what she's discovered in the desert. This great secret, which she can only haltingly speak, is her boon to the world . . . It is her gift—it is *God's* gift—to humanity.[21]

The mystic carries a vision, the prophet bears a message; the gifts of the desert are never for the individual alone. They are always for the community: "Since you are zealous for spiritual gifts, let it be for the edification of the church that you seek to excel" (1 Cor 14:12 NKJV). The message the hero brings back is nicely summarized by Hadewijch, who has known firsthand the terrors of the desert, but has also known its graces. She has some advice for those who hear the call to leave home:

> Even though those who are arid
> In faith
> Remain without surety,
> Hasten forward
> And make your way through
> Into that fat land.[22]

The Gift of Tears

Edging toward the desert? "If you have tears, prepare to shed them now." *If.* Not everyone has tears, after all; some people (mainly men, it seems) have had the ability to cry socialized out of them. Others fear that if the tears begin, they will never end. Mackenzie, the protagonist of William Paul Young's novel *The Shack*, is one of these. His daughter has been brutally murdered, and he's had a long stay in the desert of his grief. A strange invitation brings him face-to-face with the Holy Spirit, who appears to him as a mysterious woman named Sarayu:

> "Here, let me take those," her voice sang. Obviously she had not meant the coat or gun, but something else, and she was in front of him in a blink of an eye. He stiffened as he felt something sweep gently across his cheek. Without moving, he looked down and could see that she was busy with a fragile crystal bottle and a small brush, like those he had seen Nan and Kate use for makeup, gently removing something from his face.
>
> Before he could ask, she smiled and whispered, "Mackenzie, we all have things we value enough to collect, don't we?" His little tin box flashed through his mind. "I collect tears."[23]

The Bible contains a lot of references to tears. Jesus wept, as everyone knows, if only because it's the shortest verse in the Bible (John 11:35). The books of Isaiah and Revelation both contain the promise that God will wipe away all our tears (Isa 25:8; Rev 7:17; 21:4)—eventually. In the meantime, as Mack's encounter with Sarayu suggests, tears have their value; they are, in fact, one of the greatest gifts of the desert. To be sure, the desert confers this gift chiefly by kicking sand in our eyes, but the tears are no less precious for that.

The Desert Fathers and Mothers certainly placed a high value on tears. According to Isaac of Nineveh,

> he who is aware of his sins is greater than one who can raise the dead. Whoever can weep over himself for one hour is greater than the one who is able to teach the whole world; whoever

recognizes the depth of his own frailty is greater than the one who sees visions of angels.[24]

Obviously, there are tears and there are tears. Tears of self-pity, of manipulation, of emotional blackmail, are not nearly as good as raising the dead. And when depression or other illness brings tears, it should be treated, as promptly and as skillfully as possible.[25] We must relieve suffering to the degree that we can; surely life will have enough left over for our souls to work with. The tears praised by the desert ascetics are mainly of two kinds, reflecting the two faces of passion: those that come from the depth of our poverty, and those that speak of the depth of our desire. Let's look at each of these in turn.

The desert, as we have seen, forces me to face my poverty, my emptiness, my desire to live big, and give big, when in fact I am so tiny as to be barely noticeable to anyone but God. It can be a midlife thing: all the fantasies of youth, of making some kind of contribution, of "giving it all" to or for God, give way to the mature realization that I *have* nothing to give. Alan Jones remarks that "the gift of tears comes relatively late in a person's walk with God."[26] It really does take us a long time to give up on ourselves, to give in to the desert koan: "whenever I am weak, then I am strong" (2 Cor 12:10). Tears of surrender are the correct response to this koan, and they bring us to enlightenment: "One silent tear will advance us more in the spiritual way than any number of 'louder' ascetic feats or more 'visible' virtuous achievements."[27]

This poverty is a kind of death: the death of hope in ourselves. The principle of death and resurrection is so basic to the Christian faith that it's hard to know why all of this comes as such a surprise. Jesus had to be well and truly dead, after all, before he could rise, and he told us it will always be this way:

> unless a grain of wheat falls into the earth and dies, it remains just a single grain; but if it dies, it bears much fruit. Those who love their life lose it, and those who hate their life in this world will keep it for eternal life. (John 12:24-25)

The very first of the Beatitudes concerns the blessedness of poverty, and Jesus always seemed to show the greatest tenderness toward those who had come to the end of their rope: he praised the widow who gave her last few pennies, and defended the woman who had so little dignity left that she barged in where she wasn't welcome, and wept on his feet (Luke 7:36-50; 21:1-4).

Some of Christ's followers have managed to grasp this point. As I mentioned earlier, poverty is a core value of the Franciscan way, because Francis so prized the ideal of poverty that he portrayed it as a beautiful and noble lady, whom he desired above all else. His friend Clare begged the pope to grant her community the "privilege of poverty," that is, the right to own no property either individually or in common. It was a tough sell, but Clare was committed to poverty because, like Francis, she was so taken with the beauty of it:

> O blessed poverty,
>   who bestows eternal riches
>   on those who love and embrace her!
> O holy poverty,
>   God promises the kingdom of heaven
>   and, in fact, offers eternal glory and a blessed life
>   to those who possess and desire you!
> O God-centered poverty,
>   whom the Lord Jesus Christ
>   Who ruled and now rules heaven and earth,
>   Who spoke and things were made,
>   condescended to embrace before all else![28]

These two great saints, like Christ himself, placed a high value on poverty because the tears it brings erode away our resistance to God. This is the spiritual vacuum effect I spoke of earlier: poverty carves out empty space within us, and where emptiness exists, God tends to rush in. There is a story of a desert hermit whose tears over the years wore away a great hole in his chest.[29]

When I read that story, I paused and looked up on the shelf at a new icon I got in Alaska, the Virgin of the Sign. It's the one where there's a mandorla[30] at Mary's breast, in which Christ appears. She's filled with Jesus, carries him within her like a hidden light, a secret she can barely keep. It's how I want to be, and it occurred to me that negative space makes that possible. This is the mercy of the desert, to empty us of all that is taking the place of holiness, and as water seeks the lowest level, holiness seeks empty space.

We can learn to welcome tears of poverty, to know that poverty as "blessed," when we have first shed tears of desire. A young man once sought out an elder for advice on reaching enlightenment. The older man took him to a river and held his head under the water, continuing to hold him there as he struggled to break free. Finally the disciple fought his way to the surface, and gasped desperately for air. The elder looked at him and said, "Don't come to me to ask about enlightenment until you want it as much as you wanted that lungful of air."[31]

God comes to us when we need him more than we need our next breath. Most of us have gained some idea of that level of need, from observing those whose need for something completely takes over their lives. Addictions are desire gone wrong—way wrong—but they can teach us something. There are some drugs (I gather that crack cocaine is one of these) that can hook you from the very first try.[32] God is rather like crack, only a lot healthier, of course, and once you "taste and see that the LORD is good" (Ps 34:8), you will do anything, renounce anything, accept or reject anything, to taste him again. The psalms are full of expressions of this kind of desire:

> O God, thou art my God; early will I seek thee: my soul thirsteth for thee, my flesh longeth for thee in a dry and thirsty land, where no water is. (Ps 63:1)

In the desert, my heart and soul and flesh long for God, and this longing brings me to tears:

> As the hart panteth after the water brooks, so panteth my soul
> after thee, O God.
> My soul thirsteth for God, for the living God: when shall I come
> and appear before God?
> My tears have been my meat day and night, while they continu-
> ally say unto me, Where is thy God?
> When I remember these things, I pour out my soul in me. (Ps
> 42:1-4)

The poetry of the Beguine Mechthild speaks eloquently of the
tears of desire, of which she had long experience:

> Lord, two things I ask you;
> In your kindness instruct me:
> When my eyes weep in loneliness,
> And my mouth remains mute in its simplicity,
> And my tongue is constricted in affliction,
> And my senses ask me again and again
> What is wrong with me,
> Then, Lord, everything in me is directed toward you.
> When my flesh wastes away,
> My blood dries up, my bones torture me,
> My veins contract,
> And my heart melts out of love for you,
> And my soul roars
> With the bellowings of a hungry lion,
> Tell me, dearest One,
> What will it be like for me then,
> And *where will you be?*[33]

When desire reaches this point, I do indeed "pour out my soul
in me," but I often find that words don't serve me well at times
like these. Saint Paul understood this, and spoke of our inward
"groanings" as we wait for the full reality of our redemption,
for the gap between the "now" and the "not yet" to be closed
(Rom 8:22-23).[34] Paul, who knew something about deep praying (2 Cor 12:2-4), went on to explain that God has mercy on

our incoherent longing: "the Spirit helps us in our weakness; for we do not know how to pray as we ought, but that very Spirit intercedes with sighs too deep for words" (Rom 8:26).

What I'm saying is that when words fail us, God doesn't. The Spirit steps in and gives us better ways to express our desire, other languages whose vocabularies are more adequate to the task. One of these languages is tears, and when "God is felt in places too deep for words,"[35] tears have an eloquence equal to our need. In a "dry and thirsty land," tears may be the only water around, and they become an oasis where we find unexpected relief. But before they can become that, we have to accept that a consuming desire will, in fact, consume us; we have to be willing to leave the labyrinth behind, and "hurtle into the abyss."

Darkness

The idea that the ways of God are mysterious, and obscure to human understanding, is another part of the legacy Christians have received from Judaism. In Isaiah, we read:

> For my thoughts are not your thoughts, nor are your ways my ways, says the LORD. For as the heavens are higher than the earth, so are my ways higher than your ways and my thoughts than your thoughts. (Isa 55:8-9)

And when Job presumes to question God—on the reason for suffering, we should note—God turns the tables on him:

> Who is this that darkens counsel by words without knowledge? Gird up your loins like a man, I will question you, and you shall declare to me. Where were you when I laid the foundation of the earth? Tell me, if you have understanding. (Job 38:2-4)

It goes on like that for over eighty painful verses, and feels like one of those dreams where you show up for a terribly important exam, unprepared and stark naked. Job has no answer for God, but he gets the right response: "I despise myself, and repent in dust and ashes" (42:6).

The mystery of God's ways, even of God's self, continued into Christianity. The very notion of Trinity is itself a koan: how can three be one, and one three? A koan, as we saw earlier, cannot be solved; it can only be responded to, and that response, as in Job's case, is the beginning of enlightenment—light in darkness. Christians see Christ as the embodiment of enlightenment; in John's words, he is "[t]he true light, which enlightens everyone" (John 1:9). Jesus spoke often of light and darkness: "If . . . the light in you is darkness, how great is the darkness!" (Matt 6:23); "people loved darkness rather than light because their deeds were evil" (John 3:19). Jesus' use of the words "dark" and "darkness" generally carry a sinister connotation; darkness is a place of "weeping and gnashing of teeth" (Matt 8:12). Saint Paul uses the words with similar intention: "Let us then lay aside the works of darkness and put on the armor of light" (Rom 13:12).

This usage has remained with us, and perhaps it is not too far-fetched to draw a connection between these verbal images and the tendency of Christians to see darkness as something evil and menacing. (The racial implications of this tendency have been unfortunate, to say the least. Consider the expression about "the pot calling the kettle black"; black is understood as an insult.) But elsewhere in his letters, St. Paul suggests that darkness has another meaning: "For now we see through a glass, darkly" (1 Cor 13:12 KJV). Young's Literal Translation puts it this way: "for we see now through a mirror obscurely." What I am getting at here is that Christians tend to associate darkness with evil, but darkness can also carry the meaning of obscurity, of mystery. In Latin-based languages, these words are virtually interchangeable. For instance, in Italian, the word *oscurità* has all the following meanings: darkness, nighttime, obfuscation and gloom, but also obscurity and profundity.[36] This is more than a linguistic tangent. I want to suggest that when we find ourselves in darkness, we should consider the possibility that God may be doing something obscure but profound.

This is hardly a new idea, though it's one most of us seem to lose sight of when the sun goes dark and the cloud settles in on us. Indeed, when a cloud set in on the three disciples closest to Jesus, they were in the very process of seeing him more clearly than ever before. They were coming to know him more intimately than they ever had, but that knowing had an element of shadow in it: "Then a cloud overshadowed them, and from the cloud there came a voice, 'This is my Son, the Beloved; listen to him!'" (Mark 9:7). This is the paradox, this is the koan: sometimes we find the greatest clarity in the darkness; there are things we can see best in the dark. Because of this, we need to reinterpret the experience of darkness, and see it not as a sign that God has abandoned us, but as an invitation to a deeper knowing. When God draws us into dark places, we need to see that obscure movement as a call to a more intimate relationship, and a sign of God's own consuming desire.

The writer who's shed the most light on the experience of spiritual darkness is the sixteenth-century Spanish Carmelite mystic John of the Cross (though his friend, mentor, and fellow Carmelite reformer Teresa of Avila had a lot to say on the subject as well).[37] Teresa used multiple metaphors to represent the soul's journey into God, but she's best known for her image of the soul as an "interior castle," where God dwells at the center and we must make a difficult journey through successive rooms to reach him. John has the soul passing through a series of nights, in which the soul is purified and liberated from its bondage to false gods. This process is usually painful, but is necessary to prepare us for authentic relationship with the true God, that is, for the realization of our ultimate purpose.

To paraphrase John the evangelist, the world is barely able to contain the books that have been written about the work of John of the Cross on the dark night of the soul, and there is no way I can do it justice here. Instead, I will focus on three questions: First, why is the experience of darkness necessary? Second, what does the process look like? Finally, what is its result? How does the journey through dark places draw us into greater intimacy with God? This last question brings us to the subject of union, and will be taken up in the next chapter. In the remainder of this chapter, let's explore the night itself, and why it's so important to our formation.

To the soul engulfed in darkness, to say that the dark night is God's way of drawing us into deeper intimacy sounds a lot like, "This will hurt me more than it hurts you." The child has not been born who could take that statement seriously, and we too are apt to be skeptical when the mercy of God takes this brutal form. But it's our essential brokenness that makes this painful process of healing necessary, and for John of the Cross, the key to both our brokenness and our healing is *desire*, which is primarily worked out through *suffering*. For John, the spiritual journey is the ultimate love story, and in his thought, both faces of passion come into sharp focus.

The doctrine of Trinity teaches us that relationship is fundamental to God's nature: three Persons, in such intimacy that they are fully One, drawn to each other in an eternal circle of desire. And we are made of the same stuff—created in the image of God, intended for relationship, for both vertical and horizontal connection, as we saw in chapter 5. Because we're made in God's image, desire is as fundamental to our identity as it is to God's, and we too are designed to be drawn irresistibly to the Persons of the Trinity. In St. Augustine's famous words, "you have made us for yourself, and our heart is restless till it finds its rest in you." [38]

The problem is that most of us don't know how to rest in God—and probably don't even want to, because the vertical connection has been so broken. So we look for other ways to deal with our restlessness: we lose ourselves in work, or in our children. We plug the leaks with noise, with toys, with escapist TV or radio, with mindless surfing of the internet—anything to take our minds off the restless yearning, the sense of incompleteness, at our core. The seventeenth-century philosopher

Blaise Pascal described what has come to be known as the "God-shaped hole" in the human heart:

> What is it, then, that this desire and this inability proclaim to us, but that there was once in man a true happiness of which there now remain to him only the mark and empty trace, which he in vain tries to fill from all his surroundings, seeking from things absent the help he does not obtain in things present? But these are all inadequate, because the infinite abyss can only be filled by an infinite and immutable object, that is to say, only by God Himself.[39]

Nothing can fill a God-shaped hole except God, but for all kinds of reasons, we don't really want to "go there." So we plug the hole with other things, which John of the Cross called "attachments."

Attachments represent misplaced love.[40] They are the avenues of fulfillment we travel that don't lead us to God; in short, they are dead ends, but we don't realize it. Some people travel that path with a sense of desperation, while others are mostly unaware that anything significant is missing. If your attachment is a life-threatening addiction, in time it will probably get harder and harder to believe that nothing's wrong. There's a lot more cultural conditioning to support the idea of living for your career, or your kids, or just treating the odd bout of the blues with some recreational shopping. In that case, it may take a serious loss—a death, a professional or financial failure, a serious illness, or just the midlife question, "Is that all there is?"—to awaken us to our incompleteness. As we saw earlier, these are the very things that call us into the desert; they bid us leave home, and prepare for change. But home is the comfort zone, and we really don't want to leave; even if "home" isn't all that comfortable either, at least it's familiar. At least it's the devil we know.

In John's thought, what signals the onset of night is that the old things we went to—for comfort, meaning, or sheer relief—don't work anymore. Typically, our first experience of this is early in our journey, when the things of the world no longer satisfy us, and we become aware of our need for God. Of course, there are people who become aware of this need at a very early age, and it never leaves them. It's worth emphasizing that although it's tempting to turn John's ideas into a "one size fits all" stage theory, in reality people experience these things differently. But all of us have childish things we need to put away. Sometimes God rips them out of our hands, and sometimes we find they're just not that interesting anymore, and we don't know quite what to do with ourselves.

This is the "dark night of the senses," when God weans us away from the more superficial gratifications we have enjoyed in the past, and it is a relatively common experience.[41] The "dark night of the spirit" is a less common and deeper operation, in which God deals with our spiritual attachments. This night, if it comes at all, typically comes later in the journey and can feel downright catastrophic. The spiritual practices we've relied on to connect us to God don't work anymore; an accustomed sense of God's presence disappears, and we feel alone and abandoned. I remember, in a night like this, telling my spiritual director that I felt like an atheist, not because I didn't *think* God existed, but because I didn't *feel* it. And even if God did exist, it all had nothing to do with me. Sometimes the image of God a person has connected to, which seemed loving and consoling, suddenly becomes impossible, and everything goes dark. It can seem like everything one "knew"—from doctrinal certainties, to liturgy that "worked," to the very Being one called God—comes into question or disappears outright.

As if all this weren't complicated enough, John further divides each of the nights into "active" and "passive" forms. I'm not going to explore all the subtleties of these distinctions here, but the idea is that in the active nights, we're at least somewhat aware, if dimly, of what is happening, and we try to cooperate with the process. So in the active night of the senses, we will cultivate various spiritual practices (prayer, worship, spiritual reading) in place of whatever worldly things we're being weaned from. In the active night of the spirit, we'll continue trying to practice the virtues, especially the theological virtues of faith, hope, and love, even if we know we're not exactly at the top of our game.[42]

The trouble is, none of this is really going to help. As we saw earlier in the desert, we have no real weapons, and we cannot win. We are powerless over our addictions, we fail to keep our resolutions, and all our stuff just doesn't please us anymore. This is the passive night of the senses, and we begin to lose our illusions of self-sufficiency and control. In the passive night of the spirit, however, we get a long, hard look at our own poverty. The Carmelite writer John Welch provides a vivid description of this night:

> One's sins and weaknesses press in and undermine any sense of worth. Life's limitations are painfully experienced. Anxiety and bitterness spread through the soul. The fundamental trust in life's promises and one's own worth has evaporated and now no one and nothing is trustworthy. The soul experiences an intense loneliness, feeling abandoned by all; even God seems to be walking away, perhaps in anger and rejection. Prayer is all but impossible.[43]

When the darkness gets this deep, you can begin to feel like the butt of some sick cosmic joke. I pledged my life to this God, and for what? You set your own dreams aside and put your children first, and they never call. You give up a successful career to go to seminary, and your congregation is a bunch of whiners. Worse, you suspect you're not a very good pastor. I went through a painful period like this with my job in the last year, and the self-doubt can be agonizing. Or you have one health problem after another, and as you feel the limitations encroaching on you, the God you've served faithfully all your life doesn't seem to have noticed. The joke's on you, but you're not laughing. Is God?

John recognized how easy it is to confuse the dark night of the soul with depression, other illness, or the spiritually numbing effects of sin, so he gave three signs to distinguish these from the dark night.[44] First, the person going through a dark night finds "no comfort in the things of God, and none also in created things."[45] That is, all accustomed pleasures, natural or spiritual, dry up. Second, there is a "weariness" and "aridity" of spirit; the person feels unmotivated to live and serve God in their old ways. Because of this, "the soul thinks it is not serving God, but going backwards, because it is no longer conscious of any sweetness in the things of God."[46] Third, the person is unable to pray and meditate as before. Prayer has gone dark, but in some way they can't really understand (and this is critical to the task of discernment), the person is still attracted to God. It's just that it feels like an unrequited love.

Why does God do this to us? Since "God is love" (1 John 4:16), I think we can rule out "sadism" as a motivation. Essentially what God is doing is being a good parent, tearing us away from our mud pies so he can take us to Disneyland. Or, in the rather more elegant language of an anonymous fifteenth-century German mystic text:

> Learn to deny God for the sake of God—the hidden God for the sake of the unveiled God. Be willing to lose a copper coin so that you may find a golden one. Pour out water so that you may draw wine instead.[47]

Similarly, both John and Teresa see what John calls the dark night of the spirit as the transition to contemplation—that is, to a deeper union or, more accurately, to a deeper experience of the union we already have with God. The darkness is a kind of bridge between the "now" where we habitually dwell, and the "not yet" that is our destiny, the nobility for which we were born.

The trouble is that to live into that nobility, we have to grow up. We have to put away those childish things, but we're at-

tached to them. We humans are born idolaters, and the very
things God gives us to bless us and assure us of his love become
idols we worship in his stead. John puts his finger on the problem when he talks about the second sign of the dark night: the ⸎
soul "is no longer conscious of any sweetness in the things of
God." We are not only idolaters; we are also addicted to good
feelings, and we can quickly turn any sweetness associated with
God into a god itself. Remember the cycle of romantic relationships, the U-shape? In the giddy rush of infatuation, I don't
really love the other person; I love how the other person *makes
me feel*. You can't realistically talk about *love* until the relationship has survived some hard times.

Growing up is about learning to stay through the hard parts,
but it's also about learning that God stays through the hard
parts. Just as babies have to learn that objects don't disappear
when they put their hands over their eyes, we have to learn that
God is still there, even when we can't see him. It's a spiritual
version of "object permanence," and until we grasp this, we
will remain spiritual infants. Growing up is also about learning
to appreciate more subtle tastes:

> By the time life begins to break our idols, we normally find
> ourselves deadened and insensitive to the tender gifts we've been
> seeking all along. It is as if we have gorged ourselves on rich
> meals for so long that we cannot appreciate the delicate freshness
> of a sip of spring water.[48]

God has such lovely water for us, but first he's got to pry our
grubby fingers off the fizzy mix of chemicals and sugar we've
grown to love. We think we're going to die of thirst, but in
reality we just need to step away from our attachments and
submit ourselves to a bit of cleansing detox.

As painful, disorienting, and downright frightening as the
darkness can be, it is, paradoxically, a good sign. Fluent in the
language of paradox, John speaks of contemplation as a "ray of
darkness"; like the light that blinded St. Paul on the road to

Damascus, this darkening light may be our best shot at seeing clearly. As Evelyn Underhill put it, "The self is in the dark because it is blinded by a Light greater than it can bear."[49] But when the nights have done their work, and we have been freed from our attachments, both carnal and spiritual, we will be ready to live in that Light.

Again, we should beware of reducing the dark night of the soul to a formula, and expecting it to happen in a certain way. When I first started reading John of the Cross, I spent a lot of energy trying to figure out the exact order in which everything happened, and how this system squared with others (the classic mystic way of purgation, illumination, and union, Teresa's seven mansions of the interior castle, and all the rest). I imagined plotting each writer's system on a transparency, and thought that if you could lay them on top of each other and square them just so, you could see exactly what the spiritual journey would look like, and figure out precisely where you were.

Then I had a spiritual director who disabused me of that notion.[50] God is not bound to anyone's "system"; God's history with every soul is unique. And despite my reservations about some of Bernadette Roberts's work,[51] I think what she has to say on this subject is right on target:

> Authors come up with various stages, depending on the criteria they are using. St. Teresa, for example, divided the path into seven stages or "mansions." But I don't think we should get locked into any stage theory: it is always someone else's retrospective view of his or her own journey, which may not include our own experiences or insights. Our obligation is to be true to our own insights, our own inner light.[52]

The nights can come in reverse order, or repeat themselves, or overlap—each person's experience is different. That doesn't mean, however, that the movements of the soul are random, or that we're just spinning our wheels.[53] Our souls do make progress toward God, and even if we don't have exactly the same experience others had, it's nice to see footprints on the path, and the odd signpost telling us that this way is *known*.[54] In fact, it is none other than the way of the cross, and if we are traveling that way with Jesus, however much it may feel like God is lost to us, we can be sure we're not lost to God.

Despite the individual variations, relationships are pretty predictable. We can be sure that if we follow the pilgrim path long enough, we'll spend some time traveling in the dark. And when the night falls, John's counsel is very clear: don't fight it, don't panic, and don't try to make the old ways "work." Don't worry if you can't pray in the ways you're used to, or if it seems you can't pray at all. Just wait in quiet, loving attentiveness, and see what God does next. When things go dark on us, we need to remember one thing: God's purpose toward us is always love. If we can trust in that love, then we can recognize the twilight as a call to deeper intimacy, and when the night closes in on us, we can let it fold us in its arms.

Part III

Union

Chapter Nine

Coming Home:
Desire Fulfilled

Can You
Be true?
How can I believe
What I have received from Your hand?
This was not my plan.
I had hoped for just a little light,
A little lifting of the night.
Not this radiance, not this inner Sun,
This intimate, invading, dazzling One.
The liquid light that runs within my veins
Blocks out my shadows; nothing now remains
Of all my inner darkness, only this:
The lingering imprint of the soul's first kiss.
This "joining" leaves but one reality:
The fact of me in You, and You in me.

"Life is long," said Teresa of Avila, contradicting just about everyone I've ever heard. But to the soul journeying toward God, the trip can be very long indeed; as we've seen, it's full of insatiable yearning and heroic struggle, of darkness and desert, disappointment and death. If, as I claimed earlier, it's the good news that's the most true, then all this longing and loss must be leading somewhere. And it had better be good.

The Mystic Ascent: Purgation

We've seen that God's great desire is to reunite exiled souls with himself. So he plants within us a terminal case of homesickness, of *hiraeth*, a nostalgia for a homeland we lost sight of long ago. Our desire is like an inner compass, whose needle always points toward God. The problem is, somewhere along the way our compass got broken, and we forgot where our home is, or even that we had one. Most of us have humanity enough to feel compassion for senile people who wander around lost and confused. What we don't understand is that to God, we look a lot like that: going to the gas station for dinner, curling up for the night under a bridge. We are, in fact, looking for home in all the wrong places, and those places are our attachments, the false lodgings we check into because we can't find our way home.

God wants to bring us back, but as we saw when we looked at the problem of evil, force is not really his style. God is a suitor, not a rapist; there is no part of "No" that God doesn't understand. So he courts the soul through a process that has classically been broken into the stages of purgation, illumination, and union. In purgation, the soul has awakened to God, but is still mightily attached to the things of this world. For John of the Cross, the "night of the senses" is the process of relinquishment that frees us of our more tangible idols. It's a tough struggle: recall that when Moses discovered that the children of Israel had worshiped the golden calf, he melted it down and made them drink it (Exod 32). I don't know what sort of purgative melted gold makes, but as this was followed by the execution of "about three thousand of the people" (Exod 32:28), it certainly was a purgation of the ranks.

Purgation is one of those times when life does seem very long. The soul has had a glimpse of the holiness of God, and feels pretty shabby by comparison, despite all its efforts to change. As Algernon says to Jack in *The Importance of Being Earnest*, "I never saw anybody take so long to dress, and with such little result."[1] Fortunately the Spirit's work in the soul is more effective than our own, and when the process is complete, the way is cleared for the transition to illumination.

Illumination

Illumination corresponds to what Rosemary Haughton calls the "passionate breakthrough,"[2] the moment when "home" is recognized in the beloved Other:

> The response to this recognition is passion: the thrust of the whole personality towards the strange "home" it perceives. It is accompanied by intense emotion, which varies in quality according to temperament from a gentle but strong and certain joy to a desperate violence which is afraid of losing that which is perceived.[3]

These variations in temperament are important; as I said earlier, the diverse range of ways in which humans respond to the movements of God is not an inconvenience to be managed, but a richness to be cherished. So whether perceived as a gentle emptying and refilling, or an overwhelming blast of inner light, in illumination the soul is flooded with divine love. If purgation was a dry and painful time, illumination is lush and joyful, but again, how that's experienced is going to vary by personal temperament, and by the nature of the individual's call.

Indeed, God's call is surely going to be consistent with the temperament God has given. I see "apophatic" and "kataphatic" as poles on a continuum, and each individual could, in theory, be plotted somewhere on that continuum—though that position need not be permanent. Illumination is a spiritually active time, but the nature of that activity will likely depend on one's proximity to either of the poles. For Teresa of Avila, a highly emotional person who prayed with her heart on her sleeve, illumination was a time of intense feelings, of visions and voices (or "locutions"), of ecstasies and raptures. Anyone wanting to know how Teresa experienced illumination can simply look at Bernini's famous sculpture *Saint Teresa in Ecstasy*, everything she felt can be read in her face. I suspect Bernini didn't choose John of the Cross for his subject not only because women—even fully clothed—are more artistically interesting but also because John's joy, while every bit as profound, would have looked less dramatic.

It's important to note here that virtually every mystic text I've encountered cautions us not to see visions, voices, ecstasies, and other spiritual "events" (to use Janet Ruffing's term) as evidence in themselves of an advanced spiritual state. They can actually happen at any point in the journey, and can also be manufactured by one's own mind. Many people have sought these experiences, imagining them to be signs of God's favor (while others dismiss them as pointless and irrelevant at best, pathological at worst). I think such "events" can be graces, and when God gives them, it's for a purpose. But they're hardly evidence of spiritual maturity; St. Paul's encounter with Christ on the road to Damascus teaches us that much. Paul certainly experienced a significant spiritual event, involving both a vision (the light) and locution ("Saul, Saul, why do you persecute me?"), plus a supernaturally altered physical state (blindness). But since Paul was actually on his way to do violence to the infant church, it seems this most dramatic spiritual event actually occurred at the lowest point of his spiritual life. In this case, the illuminating event was actually part of the conversion experience, and was followed by a period of purgation: Paul "went away at once into Arabia" (Gal 1:17), where he seems to have spent some time letting it all percolate, and growing up enough to embark on his public ministry.

Regardless of the precise nature of the events, illumination is an eventful time, a time when the soul experiences a foretaste of union with the divine. How that experience feels, though, is again a matter of temperament and call. To the kataphatic soul, prayer can feel like being struck by slow lightning, like swallowing burning honey. It is, as a decidedly kataphatic friend of mine put it, *delicious.* The apophatic soul, on the other hand, is immersed in a silence beyond ecstasy, a silence beyond silence, not an absence of sound but a Presence too profound for words. These are extremes, however; some people will experience toned-down versions of one or the other, and some will shift between extremes in both directions. But all of these are variations on a theme, which is that the soul is moving toward a state of union with God, but has not yet arrived at that state. In Rowan Williams's words, this is

> the beginning of "spiritual betrothal"—when God and the human spirit make a conscious mutual commitment (V, 4.4). We know with new clarity who it is with whom we have to do—though the knowing is certainly not a matter of expressible conceptual clarity . . . But the betrothal is not yet formalized and finalized . . . all we have is a declaring of intentions (V, 4.5). Our *sense* of stubborn adherence is still deeply vulnerable; it is not *itself* the reality of lasting union.[4]

No, while one may experience individual *acts* of union, the "reality of lasting union"—the permanent "unitive state"—is still ahead, and will most likely be preceded by a dip back into the dark night, though this time the darkness will be deeper. Illumination is an important point on the mystic ascent, and serves an important purpose, namely, to deepen that "conscious commitment" on the human side. God gives us a glimpse of himself, but in a limited way. It's a bit like Moses asking to see God's glory, and being allowed to see only God's back as he passed by (Exod 33:18-23). It was an illuminating moment, to be sure; we read that Moses' face shone so brilliantly afterward that he had to veil himself for the sake of the people around him (Exod 34:29-35). The illumined soul nods in recognition: you can't just walk around shining all over people—they tend to find it kind of freaky. So you keep all these things, like Mary, and ponder them in your heart (Luke 2:19).

Union: The End of the Road

"The only proper end of love is union."[5] Illumination is an important and healthy stage of spiritual growth, and serves to deepen the soul's determination to reach its goal. And all of that determination is going to be needed to endure the night ahead. Still, "weeping may endure for a night, but joy cometh in the morning" (Ps 30:5). When the light finally breaks, what is that joy, that "reality of lasting union," like?

As you might expect, the apophatic and kataphatic traditions describe the unitive state in different ways. I'm inclined to think that although the language differs between the two traditions, and the experience itself feels different, the underlying process is the same: the "oneing," to use Lady Julian's word, of the soul and God. Evelyn Underhill (1875–1941), who published a comprehensive and authoritative text on mysticism at the age of thirty-six, shows how the apophatic and kataphatic descriptions of the unitive state diverge. She refers to the apophatic mystic as the "transcendent-metaphysical type," and the kataphatic as the "intimate-personal type." I think we'd better stick with apophatic and kataphatic.

The former classically describes the unitive state as *deification*, a term Underhill is quick to identify as a metaphor, not meant to be taken literally but something that points us toward a process that is "without equivalent in human speech."[6] Of course, the emphasis on the *via negativa* is on negation: God is not this, not that, no-thing, so it comes as no surprise that there's no easy vocabulary for describing apophatic union. Apophatic types are not fond of words, but when forced to speak of their experience, they like to fall back on the language of paradox ("radiant darkness") or of the absurd (the soul's "annihilation" in God). This makes it less likely that listeners will take their statements too literally, and keeps the emphasis on mystery.

Nevertheless, deification does suggest that humans can somehow become "partakers in the Divine Nature," hence the apophatic emphasis on "such symbols as those of rebirth or transmutation."[7] But Underhill does identify two frequently recurring images in this tradition that are rather more helpful to the rest of us. One is the homeland: apophatic mystics are those "by whom Reality is apprehended as a state or place rather than a Person,"[8] so there is a lot of talk of exile and homecoming. Alternatively, these writers often use the idea of fire[9]—especially of something that is, like Moses' bush, burning but not consumed. Coals and logs can be aglow with fire; the fire changes them, and they become one with it without actually becoming it. Better still (because it won't eventually be reduced to ashes), iron put in the fire is still iron, but glows with a white heat. It is transformed, changed into the likeness of fire but remains itself. These metaphors are helpful, but you can tell the writers are reaching; images are really not part of their native language.

The kataphatic fondness for imagery means that there's plenty of language to describe union. In fact, word-pictures abound in this tradition, though the ultimate symbol of kataphatic union is, as we have seen, the *spiritual marriage*. We've already spent some time with this imagery, but here is a little reminder, from Mechthild. Jesus is speaking to the soul:

> You are the feelings of love in my desire.
> You are a sweet cooling for my breast.
> You are a passionate kiss for my mouth.
> You are a blissful joy of my discovery.
> I am in you
> And you are in me.

> We could not be closer,
> For we two have flowed into one
> And have been poured into one mold.
> Thus shall we remain forever content.[10]

An interesting feature of this imagery is that, as I mentioned earlier, the unitive relationship isn't static; it keeps growing deeper. When the soul is taken by Christ as his bride, there's still plenty of passion, but the fireworks of the courtship period (illumination) tend to subside a bit, and the two settle in for the duration. When Mechthild reflects later on the "holy intimacy" of her soul with God, it's a picture of cozy domesticity:

> The soul alone with its flesh is mistress of the house in heaven, sits next to the eternal Master of the house, and is most like him. There eye reflects in eye, there spirit flows in spirit, there hand touches hand, there mouth speaks to mouth, and there heart greets heart. Thus does the Lord and Master honor the mistress at his side.[11]

It's not that the relationship has become stale—far from it. It's just become stable, grown into a tranquil closeness in which most of the drama of courtship has eased into commitment and trust. Compare Mechthild's scene with Murray Bodo's meditation on Clare of Assisi:

> Life with Jesus was a drama of finding and losing, of separation and reunion. The price you paid for ecstatic union was the loneliness and heartache of continued separation, of wondering if he had abandoned you, had ceased loving you. With the Lord, Clare experienced at times the ecstatic union of mind and heart and soul and body; the intervals between his visitations caused her more pain than she cared to think about.[12]

This is a picture of illumination, not full union. Like the woman in the Song of Songs, Clare is still afraid to let her man out of her sight, worrying that he might not come back. Let's face it:

courtship is exciting, but with all those violent emotions going *amen* on, it's kind of hard to get anything done. Mechthild's vision is quite a contrast. These two are in it for the long haul; they both know it, so now they can give their attention to other things—about which I will say more shortly. For now, though, it's worth reminding ourselves again that stage theories have their limits: darkness and delight can come and go after union has been achieved. It's just that the soul will not be jerked around by them as it was before.

Interestingly, there is a form of kataphatic imagery that, while highly affective, is not necessarily romantic or erotic in nature. This is the imagery associated with what Wendy Wright refers to as the "heart tradition," that is, the tradition of devotion to the heart of Jesus.[13] The idea that there's something of profound importance about Christ's body—that is, not just his spirit, or his mind, or teachings—is as old as Eucharist itself. Wright traces the heart's history from there through the medieval preoccupation with the wounds of Christ, and the idea that one could mystically enter Jesus' heart through the wound in his side. The heart tradition was further advanced by the visions of the seventeenth-century French Visitation nun St. Margaret Mary Alacoque.

These visions became the foundation for devotion to the "Sacred Heart" of Jesus that, as Wright points out, Catholics of a certain age will remember—possibly with affection, though there was a lot of what Donna Leon has called "chiesa [church] kitsch" in Sacred Heart imagery as well: the holy card with the fragile-looking blond Jesus holding out an apparently radio-active heart, encircled with thorns, or with tongues of flame shooting out the top. Some of it was downright creepy, at least aesthetically, and Sacred Heart devotion seems to have been one of the many that declined in the wake of the Second Vatican Council.

And yet, there is something really powerful in devotion to the heart of Christ. I mean, what else are we supposed to be devoted to, if not that? Wright considers the various forms heart imagery has taken over the centuries: the heart of Jesus as a fountain of living water; the broken heart of the crucified Christ from which water and blood (baptism and Eucharist) flowed; the heart as a refuge, as our entry point into the mystery of Godhead; a nuptial chamber, but also a table of feasting; and a fiery furnace in which all obstacles and distractions are burned away. The heart represents all of our longing, all our desire, and in the "exchange" of hearts, we see all our life in Christ, and his in us. But heart imagery is of necessity incarnational, fleshly; there is no spiritualizing this away into abstractions. In Wright's words:

> The tradition of the heart makes this vividly, even grotesquely, clear. The divine-human correspondence is intimate. It is discovered in the flesh. Our fleshly hearts are fitted for all that is beyond flesh by conforming to the heart of Jesus. That divine-human heart is the passageway between earth and heaven. That heart is the tactile tracings of divine love on the created order. That heart is the widest, wildest longing of humankind's own love.[14]

In the heart tradition, love may be romantic or not, but it is always intense, always ablaze, always just that much out of our control.

It's no surprise that the apophatic and kataphatic traditions give us two different views of the unitive state that represents the summit of the mystic ascent. In the apophatic view, union is a mystery beyond the resources of human language. The kataphatic vision makes use of our most evocative language of intimacy. Both are true, and both are inadequate. But one thing apophatic and kataphatic mystics would certainly agree on is that union is transformative; indeed, it is often referred to as "transforming union." We will come back to this point in the next chapter, but before doing so, let's pause to consider what elements of all this, if any, are relevant to ordinary people like us.

Many Are Called—But How Many?

I have spoken of the progression from purgation to union as the "mystic ascent," which raises important question: Are we all mystics? Are we all called to see this journey to the end? Clearly the beatific vision is the destiny God desires for every soul in the life to come, but what about this life? It would be nice if writers on this subject agreed on a definitive answer, but they don't. In her important work *The Silent Cry: Mysticism and Resistance*, the late German writer Dorothee Soelle opens with a chapter titled "We Are All Mystics," so I guess we know where she stood on the issue. And her attempt to "democratize" mystic experience is a healthy corrective to the long-standing tendency to view such things as the privilege of a spiritual elite, typically cloistered contemplatives and other "professional Christians," while we ordinary folk are confined to a less exalted realm. Quoting John of the Cross, Soelle claims that

> God does not reserve this high calling of contemplation for particular souls. "On the contrary, He is willing that all should embrace it. But He finds few who permit Him to work such sublime things for them."[15]

This seems to be a point on which most writers do agree: many are called, but few are chosen, because few are willing to follow the steep uphill path all the way to God. An awful lot of seed falls on stony ground, and never really grows into anything. But I also think that not everyone is called to make this journey in its entirety, at least not in this life. "Now there are varieties of gifts," says St. Paul, "but the same Spirit; and there are varieties of services, but the same Lord; and there are varieties of activities, but it is the same God who activates all of them in everyone" (1 Cor 12:4-6). People are endowed with different gifts, which equip them for different vocations. The church needs theologians to figure out what it all means. But it also needs Teresas, who insist that "the important thing is not to think much but to love much, and so to do whatever best awakens you to love." [16]

I would venture to say that every person's path probably includes some elements of mystic experience. These need not be as dramatic as visions and voices. Calmer versions of kataphatic experience include the stirring of the soul in response to a piece of music. Much apophatic activity probably goes unnoticed, simply because it is so obscure, but staring into a night sky and feeling small and quiet would certainly qualify. I think all of us are called to be attentive to these moments of mystical experience, but that is not the same thing as a mystic vocation. I'm inclined to agree with Ronald Rolheiser on this point:

> Great mystics, as is the case with artists and intellectuals, are born not made. What is important about this is that, just as the great artist or intellectual is somewhat, by nature and charism, pathologically single-minded about his or her natural area of interest, so too is the mystic. [17]

In other words, there is a kind of division of labor, or specialization, to be seen here, and the same principle is at work in all dimensions of life, including the spiritual life. Virtually all Christian congregations presumably include some kind of music in their worship, but not everyone is called to sing in the choir. God knows I don't have that particular gift, and no sane choir director would allow me to pretend I did. But although I find congregational singing in multiple parts extremely moving, and greatly enjoy it whenever it surrounds me, I'm pretty much confined to the melody myself, since I have no idea how to sing the other parts. Besides, I'm not sure what "parts" exist for someone with a vocal range of three notes.

It's the same thing with mystical experience: we're all called to go deeper in God, to meet Christ in the hidden chambers of our heart, and wait on him there with loving attention. And when we do, interesting things are likely to happen. But beyond that, some people do seem to have a certain genius for the inner life; as a result they are, as Rolheiser says, "pathologically single-minded." To expect them to be different is to ask them to extinguish their own flame: they could probably do it, but human sacrifice was never really a good idea, and still isn't. People with this gift are driven to make the ascent to the summit, cost what it may, because the smallest degree of separation between themselves and God is an unthinkable, unendurable hell.

So what exactly is a mystic, then? This is one of those things where if you ask five authorities in the area the question, you'll get at least ten answers.[18] Mysticism is notoriously hard to define. Even technical definitions range all over the place, never mind the variety of ways people use the term in ordinary speech, which often serves as a euphemism for vagueness, absentmindedness, and woolgathering. One point of consensus, however, is that mystics are emphatically *not* people who have dramatic, paranormal experiences. Plenty of genuine mystics have no such experiences, and plenty of people who do have them are just flakes.

Again, I think Rolheiser can help us here. He defines mysticism as "being touched by God in a deep inchoate way, that is, in a way that is both revelatory and authoritative, but is beyond what can be adequately conceptualized, felt, or articulated."[19] Let's take the pieces of this definition in order. The mystic is one whose soul God has touched in a way that is transformative, and unforgettable; this is why this person is so single-minded. Yet the experience is "inchoate," that is, ineffable, but inchoate also means incomplete, rudimentary. This is such an important point, because the term "mystic" tends to carry the connotation of one who is spiritually "advanced." But if mystics are born, not made, then one can be a beginner mystic, or even a lousy mystic. The term refers to a gift and a call, not a level of achievement. To say that someone is a mystic says only what path he or she has been placed on, not whether any progress has been made down that path. Mystics, too, can bury their talent in the ground.

Still, there is that deep, unforgettable touch, and it's both revelatory and authoritative. A mature mystic will have insights into the nature of God, of other humans and of creation, not by study but by a kind of intuition. The uncreated Light just makes a lot of things more clear, and that clarity brings conviction. To be sure, the fall of night can throw everything into obscurity, and the mystic who makes it to the night of the spirit will know this as painfully as anyone. But when the light returns, the soul can know with certainty what is "the better part, which will not be taken away from her" (Luke 10:42). This is the "authoritative" part: once you know God at this level, no one can easily convince you that you don't. This doesn't mean that what's been known can be explained, though there may be a strong desire to try.

Rolheiser's definition is as good as any I've come across, but I would like to make one addition to it. We have seen that desire is a fundamental part of the nature of God, and of human beings: God is attracted to us, and planted within us a deep attraction to himself. Remember the Norwegian legend about the kiss of God on each new soul, which leaves a deep memory of the One who bestowed it? All of us live with the memory of that kiss, which is the *eros*, the creative energy that drives us through life. All of us are animated by this energy, but like the Spirit who gives it, we don't necessarily realize where it came from, or where it is going. We have that little problem with the broken compass.

Thus fueled by Passion, we pursue the various passions of our lives: career, family, art and music, social justice, pets, hobbies, lusts and addictions— eros can flow through healthy and unhealthy channels. Following Rolheiser, I would say that in all of these pursuits, we indirectly pursue God:

> We wake up crying, on fire with desire, with madness. What we do with that madness is our spirituality . . . What we do with that fire, how we channel it, is our spirituality. Thus, we all have

a spirituality whether we want one or not, whether we are religious or not. Spirituality is more about whether or not we can sleep at night than about whether or not we go to church.[20]

What I am saying is that most people seek God *in* and *through* other things, that is, indirectly and often unconsciously.[21] The mystic, by contrast, seeks God directly, seeks God's own self for God's own sake. "When thou saidst, Seek ye my face, my heart said unto thee, Thy face, Lord, will I seek" (Ps 27:8). The mystic doesn't desire all kinds of things that have something of God in them; the mystic desires God. This is the "pathological single-mindedness," this is the peculiar genius of the mature mystic, and this consciousness is a direct product of the dark night. The night has stripped away all other goals, all other gods, including those false gods one made out of bits and pieces of the true God.

In this way, suffering leads ultimately to desire, and this holds true for all of us; while we can see the processes most clearly when they're most extreme, the basic principles work at all altitudes, not just the spiritual heights. The dark night frees the soul from attachment to other loves, so she can be reattached to her first love. The desert and the darkness take us to our Gethsemane, to "thy will be done": "the travail of the Dark Night is all directed toward the essential mystic act of utter self-surrender; that *fiat voluntas tua* which marks the death of selfhood in the interest of a new and deeper life."[22] The product of all this suffering is a purified desire, and that desire is itself purifying: when we will one thing with all our heart, soul, mind, and strength, we have nothing left with which to want anything else.[23]

The mystic journey is a story of passion, and it reveals both faces of passion to us. Suffering purifies and intensifies our desire, but if we follow desire far enough, if we stop covering it over, distracting ourselves from it, or scattering it among lesser gods, it will in turn lead us back to suffering:

> Those human beings who have even for a moment broken through to spheres of experience in which [Jesus] lived have suffered a longing for God so painful that it seemed, at times, that human nature could not support it. Even those less terrifyingly gifted, yet called to share to some extent in his awareness, can testify to the quality if not the degree of that pain. It is the pain of sheer love . . . There is no pain so great as the pain of the soul's longing for God. In it, all other pains are included and drawn to a point at which it is impossible to distinguish between pain and love.[24]

And so we come full circle, a circle in which desire leads to suffering, and suffering leads to desire. Actually, it's not so much a circle as a spiral, because we never return to the exact place where we began. The movement between suffering and desire is like an uphill trail with lots of switchbacks—a good thing, since none of us is tough enough to hike straight to the top. But those of us who don't have stamina enough even for the switchbacks can be heartened by the reports of those who've made it. News of the summit gives us fresh energy for the ground we'll cover today.

Fruit That Remains

So we see, finally, the two faces of passion as flip sides of each other: when suffering and desire for God are both fully realized within the soul, they become indistinguishable. When love reaches this temperature, everything melts into one. You would think that at this point, things would come to a halt, and the person would be paralyzed by bliss. A lot of people have thought this, apparently, and the idea is now known as the "heresy of quietism." This is the notion that the person in the unitive state simply folds up her wings and rests in God, in full retreat from the world. The soul just reposes on the bosom of God, in contented fulfillment, and never does anything much again.

But this vision of the end of the mystic journey is not consistent with the lives of the greatest mystics.[25] Teresa of Avila,

John of the Cross, Francis of Assisi, Paul the apostle—one could go on—all of these were not only great mystics, but either founders or reformers of great religious movements. Being active in the world seems to be a hallmark of mature spirituality, not something one leaves behind. Catherine of Genoa was a successful hospital administrator; Catherine of Siena a major political influence; and in our own time, Mother Teresa of Calcutta's tireless service to the poor was fueled by a love that was passionate, though obscure. None of these heroes of the faith reached the summit and concluded they could just lie there and do nothing. Remember Joseph Campbell's description of the hero's journey: after coming to dwell with God, you have to go home, and bring your gift back to the people.

Nor is quietism consistent with the ways in which union is conceived in either apophatic or kataphatic terms. For the apophatic mystic the goal, as we have seen, is deification, or what Thomas Aquinas calls "the last perfection": "While then a creature tends by many ways to the likeness of God, the last way left open to it is to seek the divine likeness *by being the cause of other things*."²⁶ This is the thesis of Dorothy L. Sayers's work *The Mind of the Maker*: God is creative, God is constantly in motion, bringing new things into being. We, then, are most like God, manifest the divine image most clearly, when we create—when we "cause other things"—in whatever medium we are called to work in. "My Father is always working," Jesus said, "and I too must work" (John 5:17 GNB). And so must we. I don't know if there's no rest for the wicked, but I am sure there's no rest for the blessed.

Likewise, in the kataphatic vision union is conceived of as the spiritual marriage, and only in fairy tales does the story end with the wedding. For the vast majority of couples across time and space, the normal expectation has been that marriage would eventually result in offspring. Both technology and pathology can prevent this, of course, but the fact remains that most married couples want and have children. And so it is for the spiritual marriage: Jesus assures us that if we abide in him and he in us, we will "bear much fruit" (John 15:5). This union is not going to be barren, and as delightful as the abiding is, eventually you have to get up and be about the business of "raising the family of God."[27]

Fruitfulness is expected. In fact, Jesus taught us that it's one of the core principles of discernment, of judging the quality of the relationship: "By their fruits you will know them" (Matt 7:20 NKJV). This is a critical test, *the* critical test, of a person's prayer. In Teresa's words:

> *This* is the end and aim of prayer, my daughters; *this* is the object of that spiritual marriage whose children are always good works. *Works* are the best proof that the favours which we receive have come from God . . . To give our Lord a perfect hospitality . . . Mary and Martha must combine.[28]

Evelyn Underhill emphasizes that the unitive state is marked by an influx of new energy and vitality, a life-giving creative power that brings the contemplative and active gifts of Mary and Martha together, and issues forth the wonderfully diverse fruits of the Spirit. But if that fruit is absent, she warns, however sublime a spiritual buzz we may have going, "we may be sure that we have wandered from the 'strait and narrow road' which leads, not to eternal rest, but to Eternal Life."[29] This is about as complicated a fertility test as we need. The Creator of all things isn't sterile, so if nothing's happening, we can be pretty sure the problem is on our side.

❖   ❖   ❖

This, then, is the end of the road. Union with God is our destiny; it's what we were made for, our original purpose, and our home. And until we return from exile, we will be afflicted with some degree of homesickness, though we may not call it homesickness, or even recognize it as such. Whatever language we use to describe the home we long for, whether deification, spiritual marriage, or being "immersed in an ocean of utmost peace,"[30] we can be sure that language will be inadequate to describe what Sue Monk Kidd has called "God's joyful surprise"—namely, that we are loved far beyond what we've dared to hope for, or had imagination enough to desire.

Chapter Ten

Transfiguration

> Whenever the Spirit of God breaks into our lives—in the middle of the day, in the middle of the week, or the middle of a lifetime—it is to announce in some fashion that the time for pussyfooting is over.
>
> —Brennan Manning, *The Signature of Jesus*

So mystics get to make this great heroic journey. Nice for them, but what about the rest of us? All this talk of a "deep inchoate touch" that ultimately leads to deification or the spiritual marriage, and produces fantastic outpourings of creative energy and experiences that are too wonderful to describe—well, it may seem more than a little remote to most of us. In Zeffirelli's film *Jesus of Nazareth*, a startled Mary asks the angel Gabriel, "How can this be? No one has ever touched me!" Maybe you're asking the same question. Most of us don't really have to worry about the temptation to get too comfortable at the spiritual summit; we're just hoping for enough light to get through the valley alive, and any glimpse we get of the mountains ahead is a bonus.

So let's bring things down to earth a bit. Can the likes of Teresa of Avila, John of the Cross, and other spiritual mountaineers have anything to say to those of us who are immersed in life below—busy, distracted, frightened, depressed, or just bored? I believe they can, and if they only had one word to say to us, it would be *passion*. So let's step back from the details of the spiritual journey, and take another look at the two faces of passion. First, I'd like to take a moment to recall why both suffering and desire are such critical elements of the life of faith. Then I want to reconsider how God uses both suffering and desire to form, and transform, our souls.

Passion Revisited

Authentic Christianity is a passionate faith. As we have seen, the twin themes of desire and suffering go back to our beginnings, and before our beginnings, to ancient Judaism. But Western Christianity in the twenty-first century urgently needs to see both sides of passion with greater clarity. The religious routines, partisan squabbling, and mundane daily upkeep of the institutional church often obscure the passion at the heart of the gospel. God's passionate love for humankind, and his willingness to endure suffering and death to win us back, are the core of the salvation story.

If we're paying attention, it is a dramatic, even shocking, story. In an essay called "The Greatest Drama Ever Staged," Dorothy L. Sayers considers the bizarre but undeniable reality that many people consider the teachings of Christianity to be boring. She outlines the story of the murdered God-man, and goes on to say:

> If this is dull, then what, in Heaven's name, is worthy to be called exciting? The people who hanged Christ never, to do them justice, accused Him of being a bore; on the contrary, they thought Him too dynamic to be safe. It has been left for later generations to muffle up that shattering personality and surround Him with an atmosphere of tedium. We have very efficiently pared the claws of the Lion of Judah, certified Him as

"meek and mild," and recommended Him as a fitting household
pet for pale curates and pious old ladies.[1]

Considering what the Creeds say about Jesus, she concludes
that "we may call that doctrine exhilarating or we may call it
devastating; we may call it Revelation or we may call it rubbish;
but if we call it dull, then words have no meaning at all."[2]

If we are paying attention, the gospel message is the ultimate
drama. But often we aren't paying attention; we're distracted
by the pressures and demands of our daily lives, and when we
come up for air, we face the culture wars, global warming, eco-
nomic recession, the terrorist threat at home and warfare
abroad. Physically, emotionally, and spiritually overextended,
many of us reach the point where all we ask from religion is an
hour's escape once a week from a world that threatens to over-
whelm us.

Yet when church is a place of refuge only and not a place of
challenge, of reassurance only and not of engagement with the
living God, two things will happen, neither of them good. First,
our spiritual growth gets stalled, and when we stagnate in any
area of our lives, it is likely to become boring. A steady diet of
watered-down, feel-good Christianity eventually becomes, as
William James suggested, "a dull habit" instead of the "acute
fever" it should be.[3] To taste God's presence is to thirst for
more, but the more we settle into a banal religious complacency,
the more our longing for God weakens till it becomes little
more than a ragged souvenir of youthful naïveté.

But this is an illusion. Part two of the good news is that we
are loved by a God who prefers our company to the exaltation
of heaven, and desired us more than his own earthly life. Face-
to-face with a passionate God, we find our own desire stirred
in return, till we can say with the psalmist, "my soul thirsteth
for thee; my flesh longeth for thee in a dry and thirsty land,
where no water is" (Ps 63:1). Teresa understood this; as she
said to her sisters, "I'm not asking you to do anything more
than look at Him." Looking at the "beauty of holiness"

(Ps 29:2) is bound to arouse our desire. And then, she assures us, "in the measure you desire Him, you will find Him."[4]

The second thing that happens when we fall asleep in our pews is that when life jolts us awake, we can be completely bewildered. Illness, injury, grief, unemployment, suffering, and loss of every kind throw us into dark, uncertain territory where it's hard to get our bearings. The surprise and dismay with which many greeted the revelation that Mother Teresa spent much of her life in a state of spiritual darkness suggests that the role of darkness and suffering in the spiritual life is not widely understood. We have seen how, when people find themselves in dark places, they often feel that God has abandoned them and assume they are somehow at fault: they've sinned, they aren't trying hard enough, God is fed up. If the clouds don't lift pretty quickly, they may settle into despair and a life of lowered expectations where the light, even if it does return, cannot reach them at all.

The association of darkness with abandonment is also an illusion, another desert mirage. When the Spirit drives the soul into the wilderness, into the darkness, it is so that God can "allure her," and "speak tenderly to her." The movements of God with the human soul are like an intimate dance: sometimes God steps back from us, but then draws us in closer. We need to see this process for what it is: a call to deeper intimacy, an invitation to move deeper into God. The dark night is not a necessary evil, nor is it a sign that we've lost our way. It's a necessary good, and the right way leads through this place. The night is a critical part of our transition to spiritual adulthood, and transitions can be painful: ask anyone who's given birth. But when the birthing is done, as Jesus noted (John 16:21), the pain is quickly replaced by joy.

So what do we do when darkness descends on us—how do we respond? First, we should get help with discerning what is going on. There's a kind of "uncertainty principle" in the spiritual life, which makes it very difficult to tell one's precise position, or the speed and direction of one's movement, at a given time. Mostly we can see these things clearly only in retrospect (though of course it's the premise of this book that some clue as to what's happening can be helpful). This is why competent spiritual direction, pastoral counseling, medical attention or therapy, or some combination of these, can be so helpful. If we really have lost our way, we'll need to turn back; if our chemistry is out of whack, we need to get treatment.

But if God has just stilled the wind and stalled our boat, our best bet is to simply wait it out. I have learned from a very brief experience of sailing that if the wind disappears, it doesn't make a lot of sense to stand on the deck and blow on your sail. You'll just wear yourself out, and look kind of stupid. But you also don't take the sail down and give up altogether. The best thing to do is get comfortable, pour yourself something cold, and wait for the wind to come back. It will come. And when it does, it will change everything.

Changed from Glory into Glory

In our encounter with the Beguines in chapter 4, we saw that our spooky sisters envisioned the soul undergoing a radical transformation, in which it increasingly partakes in the nature of God—what we have come to know as deification. The good news is that the ugly-duckling-turned-swan story is our story. The Bible talks a lot about our becoming "Christlike"; for example, 1 John 3:2 says, "when he is revealed, we will be like him, for we will see him as he is." When Jesus' closest friends saw him "as he was," what did they see? "And he was transfigured before them, and his face shone like the sun, and his clothes became dazzling white" (Matt 17:2). The prologue to John's gospel paints the same picture of Jesus; it's all about light, and Jesus himself taught us that we are meant to partake in this light: "if your eye is healthy, your whole body will be full of light" (Matt 6:22).

I hope I'm not guilty of egregious proof-texting, but here's how this strikes me. There's a causal argument being made here:

"we will be like him, *for* we will see him as he is." This is why Teresa asks us to "look at him"; this is why the peasant told the Curate of Ars, "I look at him, he looks at me." When we look at Jesus, that gaze, that act of looking, is transformative. When people say that prayer changes things, they clearly don't mean that prayer changes God. Although the Hebrew Scriptures occasionally portray God as changing his mind, fundamentally "I the LORD do not change" (Mal 3:6). Prayer may change circumstances, and I think this is what people usually mean when they say that prayer changes things.

But what prayer changes most is us, and it will do so most powerfully if we'll shut up and just gaze at him. That gaze is transformative; it's transfigurative, it hauls us up Mount Tabor, draws us into the arms of Christ, and bathes us in the light that was so dazzling the apostles who saw it fell on their faces in awe. It was only the three closest to Jesus who got to share that experience then, but this is the destiny of us all: "And all of us, with unveiled faces, seeing the glory of the Lord as though reflected in a mirror, are being transformed into the same image from one degree of glory to another; for this comes from the Lord, the Spirit" (2 Cor 3:18).

I think the "veil" referred to here represents all of the things that get between us and God as he really is. In other words, the veil is our attachments, and the sweaty climb up the Mount of Transfiguration is the process by which the veil is removed. And it's not just a few spiritual specialists who make this climb; this is for all of us. There are times when God simply jerks the veil away; those experiences can be shatteringly splendid, or possibly terrifying, and not all of us are subjected to them. But for most of us, most of the time, it's our gaze at God that acts like a steady, gentle tension on the veil. One day, the Bridegroom will draw the veil aside completely, and "then I will know fully, even as I have been fully known" (1 Cor 13:12).

As I said earlier, the gift of contemplation is a transformed identity. I don't believe this gift is reserved for those who are contemplatives, or mystics, by vocation. As the Spirit said to the church in Pergamum: "To *everyone* who conquers I will give . . . a white stone, and on the white stone is written a new name that no one knows except the one who receives it" (Rev 2:7; emphasis added). New names in the Bible always signify the gift of a new identity: Abram and Sarai became Abraham and Sarah, Jacob became Israel, and Simon became Peter. These names were all conferred at times of *call*, when the person was called from his or her old life to something new.

In changing a person's name, God finds a new word that communicates something to and about that person. Of course, Jesus is the Word by which the Father communicates himself completely: "in him the whole fullness of deity dwells bodily" (Col 2:9). And what is the message the Word speaks to us? "Jesus is God's Word to the world saying, 'See how I love you.'"[5] But as I mentioned in chapter 2, Rowan Williams points out that God also communicates something of himself through each of us:

> God made all things by an act of self-communication, and when we respond to his speaking, we are searching for some way of reflecting, echoing that self-communication . . . If God has made all things by the Word, then each person and thing exists because God is *speaking* to it and in it. If we are to respond adequately, truthfully, we must listen for the word God speaks to and through each element of the creation; hence the importance of listening in expectant silence.[6]

Jesus is the Word through which God's self-expression is complete. But all of us are little "words" through which God also expresses himself, and if we will listen in expectant, trusting silence, we can discover what word God is saying to the world in and through us. Then the koan will have given up its secret; then all our desert wanderings, our stumbling in the dark, our tears, and the madness of our desire, will bring us to the point where we can return home, and speak that word to the world.

Allow me one final image—one for the road. The prophet Jeremiah tells us that the souls of the redeemed "shall become like a watered garden, and they shall never languish again" (Jer 31:12). In the dark, it's easy to imagine that your soul is a vacant lot, full of litter and weeds. But if God has been at work in your soul, you can bet that some serious landscaping has been done. How do you imagine the garden of your soul? I picture a fountain at the center, which overflows and gives water to the whole garden. This, incidentally, is not far from how Teresa of Avila described the contemplative soul, or from the original plan for watering the original garden (Gen 2:5-6, 10).

Now when night begins to fall, it gets harder and harder to see the garden itself, but the fountain is lit. This just means that distractions fade, and our attention is drawn to the Source. There's no cause for alarm; we just need to pay attention, and enjoy the special magic of the evening. In deepest night, the lights of the fountain may be turned off; even the fountain itself may go quiet. At this point, we have a choice: We can panic, assuming the garden has disappeared, the fountain has wandered off, we're dead, we're damned. Or we can realize that day and night are the rhythm of life, find a hammock, and rest for a spell. And when the day returns, we'll see the garden again for what it is: a place of beauty, where God enjoys passing the time. He knows there are weeds and slugs in there; as long as a garden is planted in this earth, it's going to need tending. You don't come to a garden for the weeds and slugs, but it'd be a pretty strange gardener who'd be surprised to find them there.

So trust this gardener. Let the rhythms of the day, and the seasons of the year, take their course. Cooperate when you can, wait in quiet trust when you can't. You can't make the flowers grow, but when you discover them, you can share in God's delight. Delight is the whole point of a garden, and in due time, as the Song of Songs assures us (4:16), God will "come to his garden, and eat its choicest fruits."

Notes

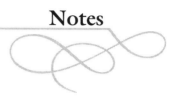

Notes to Preface, pages xv–xxi

1. Quoted in Emilie Zum Brunn and Georgette Epiney-Burgard, *Women Mystics in Medieval Europe*, translated from the French by Sheila Hughes (New York: Paragon, 1989), 161.

2. Wendy M. Wright, *Sacred Heart: Gateway to God* (Maryknoll, NY: Orbis, 2001), 2.

3. The one at the elephant's side described it as a wall, the one at the leg claimed it was a tree, while the one at the trunk said it was a snake.

Notes to Chapter One, pages 1–12

1. The Beguines were a movement of laywomen who lived lives of apostolic simplicity and service, which flourished in the thirteenth century and was being suppressed by its close. The movement produced a number of gifted mystics and poets, who can be credited with some of the earliest and finest literature in several European vernacular languages. Their work is explored in depth in chapter 4.

2. Quoted in Emilie Zum Brunn and Georgette Epiney-Burgard, *Women Mystics in Medieval Europe*, translated from the French by Sheila Hughes (New York: Paragon, 1989), 113–14.

3. Rosemary Haughton, *The Passionate God* (New York: Paulist Press, 1981), 51.

4. "Devotional Companion, with Calendar and Other Liturgical Rites" (Third Order of the Society of Saint Francis, Province of the Americas, 2004), 50.

5. Jacopone da Todi, *The Lauds* (New York: Paulist Press, 1982), 199.

6. John Michael Talbot, with Steve Rabey, *The Lessons of St. Francis: How to Bring Simplicity and Spirituality Into Your Daily Life* (New York: Plume, 1997), 230.

7. Dorothee Soelle, *The Silent Cry: Mysticism and Resistance*, trans. Barbara and Martin Rumscheidt (Minneapolis: Fortress, 2001), 113–14.

8. Ronald Rolheiser, *The Holy Longing: The Search for a Christian Spirituality* (New York: Doubleday, 1999), 4.

9. Saskia Murk-Jansen, *Brides in the Desert: The Spirituality of the Beguines* (London: Darton, Longman and Todd, 1998), 73.

10. Mechthild of Magdeburg, *The Flowing Light of the Godhead*, translated and introduced by Frank Tobin (New York: Paulist Press, 1998), 92–93.

11. Ibid., 110.

12. Quoted in Murk-Jansen, *Brides in the Desert*, 98.

13. Ibid., 72.

14. Haughton, *Passionate God*, 56.

15. Ibid., 57.

Notes to Chapter Two, pages 15–24

1. Albert Nolan, *God in South Africa: The Challenge of the Gospel* (Cape Town: D. Philip, 1988).

2. Some people would see this as humans creating God in their image: projecting all their favorite things onto an unseen being and calling it "God." I understand this, but think that if God exists, and is anything like we've been told, then all those things must come from God. It's really a causal direction debate, and since there's no way to resolve it empirically, let's move on.

3. There are many references to this throughout the New Testament, but see, for example, John 15:11; 17:21-23; Rom 8:17-18; 1 Cor 15:42-58; 2 Cor 3:18; 1 John 3:2.

4. John 14:27; 15:11.

5. Cf. Morton Kelsey, *The Other Side of Silence* (Mahwah, NJ: Paulist Press, 1997).

6. Kieran Kavanaugh, OCD, ed., *John of the Cross: Selected Writings* (Mahwah, NJ: Paulist Press), 25.

Notes to Chapter Three, pages 25–42

1. "Chocolate," from Wikipedia, accessed July 12, 2007, http://en.wikipedia.org/wiki/Chocolate.

2. "Caviar," from Wikipedia, accessed July 12, 2007, http://en.wikipedia.org/wiki/Caviar.

3. Rowan Williams, *Silence and Honey Cakes: The Wisdom of the Desert* (Oxford: Lion, 2003), 72.

4. Harvey D. Egan, *Christian Mysticism: The Future of a Tradition* (New York: Pueblo, 1984), 31, quoted in Janet K. Ruffing, "The World Transfigured: Kataphatic Religious Experience Explored through Qualitative Research Methodology," *Studies in Spirituality* 5 (1995): 236.

5. Janet K. Ruffing, RSM, *Spiritual Direction: Beyond the Beginnings* (Mahwah, NJ: Paulist Press, 2000), 96.

6. Ibid.

7. Elizabeth A. Dreyer, *Passionate Spirituality: Hildegard of Bingen and Hadewijch of Brabant* (Mahwah, NJ: Paulist Press, 2005), 38–41.

8. Ibid., 44.

9. Quoted in Rodney Stark and Roger Finke, *Acts of Faith: Explaining the Human Side of Religion* (Berkeley, CA: University of California Press, 2000), 29.

10. Ibid., introduction.

11. Sidney Callahan, *Women Who Hear Voices: The Challenge of Religious Experience* (Mahwah, NJ: Paulist Press, 2003), 16–17.

12. Ibid., 17.

13. Helena Deutsch, *The Psychology of Women: A Psychoanalytic Interpretation* (New York: Grune and Stratton, 1944), quoted in Callahan, *Women Who Hear Voices*, 18.

14. Callahan, *Women Who Hear Voices*, 8. Her quotation is from Amy Hollywood, *Sensible Ecstasy: Mysticism, Sexual Difference, and the Demands of History* (Chicago: University of Chicago Press, 2002), 5.

15. Callahan, *Women Who Hear Voices*, 113.

16. Following Keating, I use these terms interchangeably: Thomas Keating, *Open Mind, Open Heart: The Contemplative Dimension of the Gospel* (New York: Continuum, 1997), 146–47.

17. Technically, this is "infused contemplation," contemplation that is received, not achieved.

18. Keating, *Open Mind, Open Heart*, 146.

19. "Discursive meditation" involves reflecting on the passage, visualizing the events in the mind's eye, considering the lessons contained in it, and applying them to one's own life.

20. Keating, *Open Mind, Open Heart*, chap. 2.

21. Janet K. Ruffing, "The World Transfigured: Kataphatic Experience Explored through Qualitative Research Methodology," *Studies in Spirituality* 5 (1995): 233.

22. Ibid.

23. Keating, *Open Mind, Open Heart*, 21.

24. Quoted in Callahan, *Women Who Hear Voices*, 9.

25. Keating, *Open Mind, Open Heart*, 25.

26. Brennan Manning, *The Signature of Jesus: A Path to Living a Life of Holy Passion and Unreasonable Faith* (Sisters, OR: Multnomah, 1996), 205.

27. Ibid., 83.

28. Ibid., 29.

29. Ruffing, "World Transfigured," 232–33.

30. Ibid., 232.

31. Ibid.

32. Ibid., 234.

33. Ibid., 95; Dreyer, *Passionate Spirituality*, 56–57.

34. This section on the Song of Songs relies heavily on two texts: Dorothee Soelle, *The Silent Cry: Mysticism and Resistance*, trans. Barbara and Martin Rumscheidt (Minneapolis: Fortress, 2001), 116–18; and Tara Soughers, *Falling in Love with God: Passion, Prayer, and the Song of Songs* (Cambridge, MA: Cowley, 2005), chap. 2.

35. Soughers, *Falling in Love with God*, 18–19.

36. Quoted in ibid., 19.

37. The historicity of this event, reported by Eusebius, is not universally accepted.

38. Quoted in Dreyer, *Passionate Spirituality*, 43.

39. *Book of Common Prayer* (New York: Oxford University Press, 1979), 423.

40. Soughers, *Falling in Love with God*, 21–22.

41. Quoted in Soelle, *Silent Cry*, 117.

42. Dreyer, *Passionate Spirituality*, 66.

43. Quoted in Soelle, *Silent Cry*, 117.

44. Emilie Zum Brunn and Georgette Epiney-Burgard, *Women Mystics in Medieval Europe*, translated from the French by Sheila Hughes (New York: Paragon, 1989), xxv–xxix.

Notes to Chapter Four, pages 43–61

1. Carolyn Walker Bynum, *Jesus as Mother: Studies in Spirituality of the High Middle Ages* (Berkeley: University of California Press, 1980), 14.

2. For background on the Beguine movement, I am greatly indebted to Saskia Murk-Jansen's book *Brides in the Desert: The Spirituality of the Beguines* (London: Darton, Longman and Todd, 1998); as well as to Marygrace Peters, OP, "The Beguines: Feminine Piety Derailed," *Spirituality Today* 43, no. 1 (Spring 1991): 36–52; and to Elizabeth T. Knuth, whose article "The Beguines" (1992) may be found at www.users.csbsju.edu/~eknuth/xpxx/beguines.html.

3. The origins of the name "Beguine" are uncertain. It has been linked to Lambert le Begue and Jehans li Beguins, both from Liege, where the movement arose, as well as the word "Albigensian," which accounts for its association with heresy, and could also be related to "begging," a practice that developed later in the movement and attracted considerable criticism (Murk-Jansen, *Brides in the Desert*, 26–27; Knuth, "Beguines," 1).

4. The movement also included a small number of men, known as "Beghards."

5. At that time, texts on spiritual matters were typically written in Latin, which limited their audiences mainly to clergy, religious, and scholars. For such writings to be more widely accessible tended to make ecclesial authorities nervous.

6. R. W. Southern, *Western Society and the Church in the Middle Ages* (New York: Viking, 1970), 330, quoted in Peters, "Beguines: Feminine Piety," 7–8.

7. Knuth, "Beguines," 4.

8. Murk-Jansen, *Brides in the Desert*, 123, fn. 32.

9. In the following section I am greatly indebted to two studies of the Beguines, Saskia Murk-Jansen's *Brides in the Desert*, and Emilie Zum Brunn and Georgette Epiney-Burgard's *Women Mystics in Medieval Europe*, translated from the French by Sheila Hughes (New York: Paragon, 1989). Each of these books provides an excellent and accessible introduction to the Beguines, their movement and their characteristic spirituality.

10. Zum Brunn and Epiney-Burgard, *Women Mystics in Medieval Europe*, 196, fn. 1.

11. Murk-Jansen, *Brides in the Desert*, 76.

12. Mechthild of Magdeburg, *The Flowing Light of the Godhead*, translated and introduced by Frank Tobin (Mahwah, NJ: Paulist Press, 1998), 96.

13. Ibid., 96.

14. Ibid., 72.

15. Zum Brunn and Epiney-Burgard, *Women Mystics in Medieval Europe*, 51.

16. Murk-Jansen, *Brides in the Desert*, 47.

17. Ibid., 91.

18. Ibid., 90–94.

19. *Hadewijch: The Complete Works*, translation and introduction by Mother Columba Hart, OSB (Mahwah, NJ: Paulist Press, 1980), 294.

20. Quoted in Zum Brunn and Epiney-Burgard, *Women Mystics in Medieval Europe*, 91–92.

21. Ibid., 183.

22. *Hadewijch: The Complete Works*, 281.

23. Mechthild, *Flowing Light of the Godhead*, 93–94.

24. Hadewijch: The Complete Works, 139.

25. Mechthild, *Flowing Light of the Godhead*, 287.

26. Wendy M. Wright, *Sacred Heart: Gateway to God* (Maryknoll, NY: Orbis, 2001).

27. Janet K. Ruffing, RSM, *Spiritual Direction: Beyond the Beginnings* (Mahwah, NJ: Paulist Press, 2000), 125.

28. Mechthild, *Flowing Light of the Godhead*, 61–62.

29. Rodney Stark and Roger Finke, *Acts of Faith: Explaining the Human Side of Religion* (Berkeley, CA: University of California Press, 2000).

30. Ronald Rolheiser, *The Holy Longing: The Search for a Christian Spirituality* (New York: Doubleday, 1999), 15–16.

31. C. S. Lewis, *The Weight of Glory and Other Addresses* (New York: Touchstone, 1975), 36.

32. Jessica Boynton, "Welsh Language and Culture," research paper, accessed August 13, 2007, http://people.emich.edu/jboynton/research/welsh.html.

33. Ps 121:8.

34. Susan Pitchford, *Following Francis: The Franciscan Way for Everyone* (Harrisburg, PA: Morehouse, 2006), 26–27.

35. C. S. Lewis, *Letters to Malcolm: Chiefly on Prayer* (San Diego, CA: Harvest, 1992), 89.

36. Quoted in Zum Brunn and Epiney-Burgard, *Women Mystics in Medieval Europe*, 92.

37. Ibid., 105.

38. Quoted in ibid., 105.

39. Mechthild, *Flowing Light of the Godhead*, 87.

40. Zum Brunn and Epiney-Burgard, *Women Mystics in Medieval Europe*, 155.

41. Quoted in ibid., 154.

42. Dom J.-B. Porion, quoted in ibid., xix.

Notes to Chapter Five, pages 62–84

1. Cathy Lynn Grossman, "Charting the Unchurched in America," *USA Today*, March 7, 2002, http://www.usatoday.com/life/2002/2002-03-07-no-religion.htm.

2. Aimee Heckel, "More Describe Selves as Spiritual, Not Religious," DailyCamera.com, Boulder, CO, April 27, 2008, accessed May 9, 2009, http://www.dailycamera.com/ci_13095951?IADID=Search-www.dailycamera.com-www.dailycamera.com. Quoted statements are reader responses to the article.

3. Cf. Matt 20:1-16.

4. Thanks to Judith Gillette for this insight.

5. Ronald Rolheiser, *The Holy Longing: The Search for a Christian Spirituality* (New York: Doubleday, 1999), 33–35.

6. Ibid., 34.

7. Dear Mom and Dad: I was never into casual sex. Please resume breathing now.

8. Susan Pitchford, *Identity Tourism: Imaging and Imagining the Nation* (Bingley, UK: Emerald), 68–71.

9. Jason Brown, profile, "About Me," accessed May 18, 2009, http://people.tribe.net/punksonis.

10. Ibid.

11. Mary Waters, *Ethnic Options: Choosing Identities in America* (Berkeley, CA: University of California Press, 1990).

12. Ibid.

13. Jean Noël Vuarnet, *Exstases Féminines* (Paris: Arthaud, 1980), 77, quoted in Paul Lachance, OFM, *Angela of Foligno: Complete Works* (Mahwah, NJ: Paulist Press, 1993), 101.

14. Lachance, *Angela of Foligno*, 16–18.

15. Ibid., 141, 143.

16. 1 Cor 13:6.

17. US Immigration and Customs Enforcement.

18. Janet K. Ruffing, RSM, *Spiritual Direction: Beyond the Beginnings* (Mahwah, NJ: Paulist Press, 2000), 111; emphasis added.

19. Ibid., 126.

20. Elizabeth Barrett Browning, Sonnet 22.

21. Ezek 36:26.

22. Elizabeth A. Dreyer, *Passionate Spirituality: Hildegard of Bingen and Hadewijch of Brabant* (Mahwah, NJ: Paulist Press, 2005), 141.

23. For an in-depth analysis of acedia, see Kathleen Norris, *Acedia and Me: A Marriage, Monks, and a Writer's Life* (New York: Riverhead, 2008).

24. Deborah Smith Douglas, "Staying Awake," *Weavings* XVII, no. 4 (July/August 2002): 39.

25. Luke 10:42 Holman.

26. Matt 25.

27. Ibid.

28. Quoted in Dreyer, *Passionate Spirituality*, 121.

29. Wendy Farley, *The Wounding and Healing of Desire: Weaving Heaven and Earth* (Louisville, KY: Westminster John Knox Press), 16.

30. Rom 8:26.

31. Sonnet 22.

Notes to Chapter Six, pages 87–97

1. Scott Conroy, "5 Kids Die In Pittsburgh House Fire," CBSNews.com, June 12, 2007, http://www.cbsnews.com/stories/2007/06/12/national/main2918032.shtml.

2. Apparently there was no babysitter. A follow-up story published nearly a year later reported that the two mothers, both in their mid-twenties, had left the younger children in the care of the eight-year-olds while they spent the evening at a local tavern. Both women were convicted on multiple counts of involuntary manslaughter; one was also convicted of making a false report to the police concerning the nonexistent babysitter. Gabrielle Banks, "Mothers Sentenced in Deaths of 5 Children in Larimer Fire," post-gazette.com, May 22, 2008, http://www.post-gazette.com/pg/08143/883978-100.stm.

3. Kevin Bales, *Disposable People: New Slavery in the Global Economy* (Berkeley, CA: University of California Press), 1–2.

4. The biopsy was negative—God is off the hook this time.

5. David Rensberger, OEF, "Suffering Together before God," *Weavings* 17, no. 5 (September/October 2002): 39–40.

6. Mary Whiting, sermon delivered on June 17, 2007.

Notes to Chapter Seven, pages 98–116

1. Wrongly, as it turned out, but it felt good at the time.

2. Robert Harrison, *Oriel's Diary: An Archangel's Account of the Life of Jesus* (Bletchley, UK: Scripture Union, 2002).

3. Walter Wangerin, *Jesus* (Oxford: Lion, 2005).

4. Emphasis obviously added—they didn't have italics in those days.

5. "Myanmar Agrees to Accept ASEAN Cyclone Aid," CNN.com, accessed May 19, 2008, http://www.cnn.com/2008/WORLD/asiapcf/05/19/myanmar.aid/index.html.

6. "Aftershock Triggers Slides at Quake Epicenter," msnbc.com, May 16, 2008, http://www.msnbc.msn.com/id/24642170/.

7. Italics in the original.

8. Elaine M. Prevallet, SL, "Carrying in the Body the Death of Jesus," *Weavings* XVII, no. 5 (September/October 2002): 19. Prevallet goes on to consider a deeper meaning to the term; I will return to this meaning later.

9. Phil 2:12.

10. 2 Cor 4:8-11: "We are afflicted in every way, but not crushed; perplexed, but not driven to despair; persecuted, but not forsaken; struck down, but not destroyed; always carrying in the body the death of Jesus, so that the life of Jesus may also be made visible in our bodies. For while we live, we are always being given up to death for Jesus' sake, so that the life of Jesus may be made visible in our mortal flesh."

11. For a summary of cauda equina syndrome, see http://www.emedicinehealth.com/cauda_equina_syndrome/article_em.htm, accessed July 2, 2008.

12. My husband, I hasten to add, is not one of these.

13. The words are from the celebration of a marriage in the *Book of Common Prayer* (New York: Oxford University Press, 1979), 423.

14. I want to emphasize again that God has *allowed* my present suffering; he has not *caused* it. And clearly, we are allowed to suffer whether we give our consent or not. But in speaking of "God's will," theologians have distinguished between what God actually wants for us and what God will tolerate on the way to the final restoration of his broken world. To accept that the anguish of millions of Chinese and Burmese makes sense in the light of a larger divine plan takes some believing, and I doubt I can talk anybody into that kind of faith. But somehow I believe it, and it helps me accept not only the distant suffering of people I'll never know, but my own, all-too-familiar loneliness, anxiety, and pain.

15. To be fair to Peter, his statement did improve as he kept talking: "You have the words of eternal life. We have come to believe and know that you are the Holy One of God" (John 6:68-69).

16. *Principles of the Third Order of the Society of Saint Francis*, Day 27. See http://tssf.org/principles.shtml.

17. Prevallet, "Carrying in the Body," 21.

18. I have described that struggle in *Following Francis: The Franciscan Way for Everyone* (Harrisburg, PA: Morehouse, 2006).

19. I am indebted to Frank Shirbroun, whose sermon on that occasion (July 20, 2008) helped me apply the Scriptures to my situation.

20. Ps 139:7-12.

21. Meister Eckhart, quoted in Thomas E. Pullyblank, "Out of the Depths We Cry: How Christian Prayer Responds to Pain, Suffering and Evil," accessed August 26, 2010, http://spiritualityandhistory.com/Chapter%20Three:%20Common%20Responses%20to%20Pain,%20Suffering%20and%20Evil.html.

Notes to Chapter Eight, pages 117–43

1. Ronald Rolheiser, OMI, "John and Human Development: 'The Dark Night of the Soul . . . A Contemporary Interpretation,' " accessed July 31, 2010, http://www.ronrolheiser.com/common/pdf/joc_human_dev.pdf.

2. The Septuagint is the Greek translation of the Hebrew Scriptures produced in the third and second centuries BCE. The Vulgate is the Latin translation of the Bible, mainly produced by St. Jerome in the fourth century.

3. James Howlett, "Desert (in the Bible)," *The Catholic Encyclopedia*, vol. 4 (New York: Robert Appleton Company, 1908), September 15, 2010, http://www.newadvent.org/cathen/04749a.htm.

4. Abraham J. Heschel, *The Prophets* (New York: Perennial, 2001 [1962]), 70–73.

5. Gen 4:1.

6. John Chryssavgis, *In the Heart of the Desert: The Spirituality of the Desert Fathers and Mothers* (Bloomington, IN: World Wisdom, 2008), 33–34.

7. It is, however, beautifully imagined in Anne Rice's *Christ the Lord: The Road to Cana* (Toronto: Knopf, 2008).

8. Kerry Walters, *Soul Wilderness: A Desert Spirituality* (Mahwah, NJ: Paulist Press, 2001), chap. 1.

9. Alan Jones, *Soul Making: The Desert Way of Spirituality* (New York: HarperOne, 1989), 69–73.

10. Ibid., 72–73; emphasis in the original.

11. Walters, *Soul Wilderness*, 85.

12. Chryssavgis, *In the Heart of the Desert*, chap. 2.

13. David Rensberger, "Deserted Spaces," *Weavings* XVI, no. 3 (May/June 2001): 10.

14. Saskia Murk-Jansen, *Brides in the Desert: The Spirituality of the Beguines* (London: Darton, Longman and Todd, 1998), chap. 5.

15. Hadewijch of Brabant, quoted in Murk-Jansen, *Brides in the Desert*, 103.

16. M. Robert Mulholland Jr., "Life In the Desert," *Weavings* XVI, no. 3 (May/June 2001): 23.

17. Charles Dickens, "A Christmas Carol," *A Christmas Carol and Other Christmas Books* (New York: Everyman's Library, 2009), 21.

18. Walters, *Soul Wilderness*, 3–6.

19. Quoted in Chryssavgis, *In the Heart of the Desert*, 41.

20. Rowan Williams, *Silence and Honey Cakes: The Wisdom of the Desert* (Oxford: Lion, 2003), 84; emphasis added.

21. Walters, *Soul Wilderness*, 10; emphasis in the original.

22. Quoted in Murk-Jansen, *Brides in the Desert*, 105.

23. William Paul Young, *The Shack* (Newbury Park, CA: Windblown Media, 2007), 84.

24. Quoted in Jones, *Soul Making*, 82.

25. I am in full agreement with Gerald May on this point; see Gerald G. May, *The Dark Night of the Soul: A Psychiatrist Explores the Connection Between Darkness and Spiritual Growth* (San Francisco: HarperSanFrancisco, 2004). While God can turn any life circumstances to our spiritual benefit, failing to treat depression or any other illness on the grounds that treatment would interfere with God's work is inhumane, and betrays criminal ignorance of both psychology and the Christian faith.

26. Jones, *Soul Making*, 103.

27. Chryssavgis, *In the Heart of the Desert*, 49.

28. Clare of Assisi, The First Letter to Agnes of Prague, quoted in Claire Marie Ledoux, *Clare of Assisi: Her Spirituality Revealed in Her Letters*, trans. Colette Joly Dees (Cincinnati, OH: St. Anthony Messenger, 1997), 32–33.

29. Chryssavgis, *In the Heart of the Desert*, 48.

30. An almond-shaped space ("mandorla" is Italian for "almond"), frequently used in iconography, in which Christ or saints are placed.

31. Jones, *Soul Making*, 86.

32. I'm not sure that first-exposure addiction is supported by research, but it is popularly believed.

33. Mechthild of Magdeburg, *The Flowing Light of the Godhead*, translated and introduced by Frank Tobin (Mahwah, NJ: Paulist Press, 1998), 94–95; emphasis added.

34. The "now" referred to here is the work of God already completed in us; the "not yet" is the full realization of that work. So our redemption has been accomplished by Christ, is complete "now," but the full coming of the kingdom, and our full participation in the life of resurrection, is "not yet."

35. Jones, *Soul Making*, 84.

36. WordReference.com, Online Language Dictionaries, accessed July 30, 2010, http://www.wordreference.com/iten/oscurità.

37. In the discussion of John and Teresa that follows, I draw heavily from three main sources: John Welch, OCarm, *The Carmelite Way: An Ancient Path for Today's Pilgrim* (Mahwah, NJ: Paulist Press, 1996); May, *Dark Night of the Soul*; and Ronald Rolheiser, OMI, "John of the Cross—The Man, the Myth, and the Truth," accessed July 31, 2010, http://www.ronrolheiser.com/common/pdf/joc_man.pdf.

38. Saint Augustine, *The Confessions* (New York: Everyman's Library, 2001), 5.

39. Blaise Pascal, *Pensées*, section VII, 425.

40. May, *Dark Night of the Soul*, 51.

41. Ibid., 80–81.

42. Ibid., chap. 3.

43. Welch, *Carmelite Way*, 73.

44. John of the Cross, *The Dark Night of the Soul & The Living Flame of Love* (London: Fount Classics, 1995), chap. IX.

45. Ibid., 36.

46. Ibid.

47. Quoted in Dorothee Soelle, *The Silent Cry: Mysticism and Resistance*, trans. Barbara and Martin Rumscheidt (Minneapolis: Fortress, 2001), 83.

48. May, *Dark Night of the Soul*, 151.

49. Evelyn Underhill, *Mysticism: A Study in Nature and Development of Spiritual Consciousness* (Stillwell, KS: Digireads, 2005 [1911]), 269.

50. Thanks to Valerie Lesniak for teaching me this.

51. I'm not an expert on Bernadette Roberts, but I'm inclined to think that when she speaks of a stage "beyond union," what she's

really describing is a process of moving deeper *in* union. After all, God is infinite; it's not like you can pass through God and get to the "other side." The other side of God is God.

52. From an interview with Stephan Bodian, which appeared in the November/December 1986 issue of YOGA JOURNAL, reprinted at http://webcache.googleusercontent.com/search?q=cache:xL25FQ9_kT4J:www.spiritualteachers.org/b_roberts_interview.htm+bernadette+roberts+interview+retrospective&cd=1&hl=en&ct=clnk&gl=us, accessed August 12, 2010.

53. May, *Dark Night of the Soul*, 127.

54. Ibid., 95.

Notes to Chapter Nine, pages 147–65

1. Oscar Wilde, *The Importance of Being Earnest,* in *Oscar Wilde: The Major Works*, ed. Isobel Murray (Oxford: Oxford University Press, 1989), 511.

2. Rosemary Haughton, *The Passionate God* (New York: Paulist Press, 1981), 50–51.

3. Ibid., 60.

4. Rowan Williams, *Teresa of Avila* (London: Continuum, 1991/2002), 129; emphases in the original.

5. Evelyn Underhill, *Mysticism: A Study in Nature and Development of Spiritual Consciousness* (Stillwell, KS: Digireads, 2005 [1911]), 289.

6. Ibid., 283.

7. Ibid.

8. Ibid.

9. Ibid., 284–85.

10. Mechthild of Magdeburg, *The Flowing Light of the Godhead*, translated and introduced by Frank Tobin (Mahwah, NJ: Paulist Press, 1998), 111.

11. Ibid., 157–58.

12. Murray Bodo, *Clare: A Light in the Garden* (Cincinnati, OH: St. Anthony Messenger, 1992), 19–20.

13. Wendy M. Wright, *Sacred Heart: Gateway to God* (Maryknoll, NY: Orbis, 2001). Wright actually traces the heart tradition back to its earlier roots in the Hebrew Scriptures, e.g., Ezekiel 36:26: "A new heart I will give you, and a new spirit I will put within you; and I will remove from your body the heart of stone and give you a heart of flesh."

14. Ibid., 48.

15. Dorothee Soelle, *The Silent Cry: Mysticism and Resistance*, trans. Barbara and Martin Rumscheidt (Minneapolis: Fortress, 2001), 14.

16. Teresa of Avila, *Interior Castle*, trans. E. Allison Peers (New York: Doubleday, 1961).

17. Ronald Rolheiser, OMI, "John of the Cross—The Man, the Myth, and the Truth," accessed July 31, 2010, http://www.ronrol heiser.com/common/pdf/joc_man.pdf.

18. The same is true for the term "contemplative." There are any number of technical definitions of this term, but a simple one that works for me is this: A contemplative is one who feels drawn to spend a lot of time alone with God, and whose prayer includes but goes beyond confession, petition, and intercession. A contemplative will spend a good bit of his or her prayer life in adoration and oblation (offering oneself to God), that is, in prayer that transcends words. As a contemplative grows, prayer increasingly becomes continuous, and saturates the whole of that person's life.

19. Rolheiser, "John of the Cross."

20. Ronald Rolheiser, *The Holy Longing: The Search for a Christian Spirituality* (New York: Doubleday, 1999), 7.

21. It's not my intention to baptize the unwilling here, to make spiritual seekers of those who want nothing to do with spiritual things. But I do believe that the passion in the life of the most determined atheist comes from God. If all things come from God, then it follows that this also does. If all things don't come from God, then everything else I've said in this book is wrong too. Maybe they'll give you your money back.

22. Underhill, *Mysticism*, 278.

23. This doesn't mean that when we desire God perfectly, we will desire nothing and no one else. It's just that when we fulfill the first great commandment to love God with all we are and all we have, all other loves will assume their proper places in our lives. We will love others rightly and well, and avoid the tendency to turn them into idols.

24. Haughton, *Passionate God*, 151.

25. Underhill, *Mysticism*, 295.

26. Quoted in ibid., 289; emphasis added.

27. John Michael Talbot, *The Lover and the Beloved: A Way of Franciscan Prayer* (New York: Crossroad, 1985), 83.

28. Quoted in Underhill, *Mysticism*, 290; emphases in the original.

29. Ibid.

30. Catherine of Genoa, quoted in ibid., 298.

Notes to Chapter Ten, pages 166–73

1. Dorothy L. Sayers, *Creed or Chaos?* (Manchester, NH: Sophia Institute, 1974), 6.

2. Ibid., 8.

3. "In some, says William James, religion exists as a dull habit, in others as an acute fever" (Thomas R. Kelly, *A Testament of Devotion* [San Francisco: HarperSanFrancisco, 1992 (1941)], 27).

4. Quoted in John Welch, OCarm, *The Carmelite Way: An Ancient Path for Today's Pilgrim* (Mahwah, NJ: Paulist Press, 1996), 66.

5. Brennan Manning, *The Signature of Jesus: A Path to Living a Life of Holy Passion and Unreasonable Faith* (Sisters, OR: Multnomah, 1996), 155.

6. Rowan Williams, *Silence and Honey Cakes: The Wisdom of the Desert* (Oxford: Lion, 2003), 72; emphasis in the original.

Index

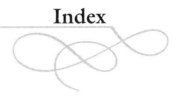